CW00594924

Rita F. Snowden is wid[...] [...] the author of more than 60 books for adu[...] After six years in business she trained as a deaconess of the New Zealand Methodist Church, serving in turn two pioneer country areas before moving to the largest city for several years of social work during an economic depression.

Miss Snowden has served the world Church, beyond the ministry of her own denomination, with regular broadcasting commitments. She has written and spoken in Britain, Canada and the United States, and in Tonga at the invitation of Queen Salote. She has represented her church at the World Methodist Conference in Oxford, later being elected the first woman Vice-President of the New Zealand Methodist Church, and President of its Deaconess Association. She is an Honorary Vice-President of the New Zealand Women Writers' Society, a Fellow of the International Institute of Arts and Letters, and a member of P.E.N.

Miss Snowden has recently been honoured by the award of the Order of the British Empire, and by the citation of 'The Upper Room' in America.

Her most recent books are *Prayers for Busy People*, *Christianity Close to Life* and *Bedtime Stories and Prayers*.

RITA F. SNOWDEN

I BELIEVE
HERE AND NOW

I believe in Christianity, as I believe that the sun has
risen, not only because I see it, but because by it I
see everything else.

C. S. Lewis

COLLINS
Fount Paperbacks

First published in Great Britain
in 1981 by Fount Paperbacks

© Rita F. Snowden 1981

Made and printed in Great Britain by
William Collins Sons & Co Ltd, Glasgow

For
my Scottish friend Isabel

CONTENTS

INTRODUCTION

Few of us these days skip out lightly to bring in the morning paper. We find it rather painful to live in the present tense. We can believe that God did glorious things for our fathers; but darkness is so real in this age, and is of so many types.

One unforgettable morning, circling the earth, I wakened in Cologne, its ancient cathedral piercing the sky. It was Sunday; and with my home-sharing friend I went to worship. For all that I did not know German, I felt myself, in a very real way, part of that vigorous congregation, all standing save for a fringe of aged folk and nursing-mothers occupying the few seats provided.

Several years later, I was back in Cologne. Meanwhile, dictators masquerading as men of destiny had reaped a harvest of hate. And the footprints of fear were still in the earth. In Cologne, the cathedral had suffered grievous damage. But whilst in the city, I learned of a happening during its past dark days. Seven Jewish refugees with their pitiful little bundles had sheltered beneath the cathedral, at the invitation of one of another creed – the Archbishop of Cologne. And there, reaching up out of their dark experience, they scratched on the wall words that spoke for each:

I believe in the dawn, though it be dark;
I believe in God, even though He be silent.

Those words inspired me – and they inspire me still. Along with joy, and satisfaction in friendship, work and home, I have to admit to knowledge of the world's headlines; to an experience of grave illness; to death in my family; to shared suffering with neighbours; a medical diagnosis issuing in cancer for my closest friend; an experience of shame, shared with a little company linked by ties of community and acknowledged responsibility.

But '*I believe*. . .' and now associate closely those words from Cologne with the nineteenth and twentieth chapters of St John's Gospel, with those experiences which make up my life. For these chapters proclaim a triumphant scattering of darkness. The crucifixion chapter leads on immediately to the striking opening of the next chapter: 'The first day of the week cometh Mary Magdalene early, *when it was yet dark* . . . unto the sepulchre, and seeth the stone rolled away.' Even before Mary could come hastening with her burial spices and her grief, God was there, banishing the dark.

We need, each of us – if what we are passing through is to be handled well – the persuasive reality of the Open Tomb in the Easter Garden. For always – even to this hour – God is at work! This, surely, has never been better expressed, outside the gospels themselves, than by Scotland's loved preacher, Dr James S. Stewart of our day: 'Remember that this world, which has the tears of Calvary in it,' says he, 'has also the songs of Easter! Today, there may seem to be nothing for you but sheer naked faith, fighting doggedly against terrific odds of doubt; *but God does not mock His children with a night that has no ending; and to everyone who stands resolute while the darkness lasts*, there comes at length the vindicating of the faith, and the breaking of the day!'

> 'I believe in God
>   The Father Almighty,
>   Maker of Heaven and earth:
> And in Jesus Christ
>   His only Son our Lord . . . !'

I BELIEVE . . . IN GOD'S WORLD

I have circled this world that I know, several times. And its challenge is gathered up for me in a geographical replica on the communion table in a Presbyterian Church in our city. Several times I have been privileged to lead worship in St David's; and always that globe has checked me – so that now I can more sincerely and deeply say: '*I believe in God's world!*'

This world that we know, and God Himself, are inseparably linked in Creation, and in Love. His incarnational act gloriously effected that. Our best-known verse in the whole of Scripture celebrates it: '*God so loved the world*, that He gave His only begotten Son, that whosoever believeth in Him should not perish, but have everlasting Life' (John 3:16. A.V.).

And this remains God's world, though we have done evil and dark things within it. Daily, our newspapers gather up these deeds in reportage, to furnish striking headlines. But God has many other ways of stabbing our spirits broad-awake. Sometimes it is one thing, sometimes another – a sunrise, a sunset, or some extraordinary beauty; a mountain height aspiring, an act of self-forgetfulness, or a moment of silent meditation. It was one quiet moment that challenged a woman of faith some while back, who shared her experience with me. Facing each one in a city Meeting of Quakers, was a large six-paned window, made up of five opaque panes, and one of clear glass – a damaged pane, repaired. 'Every time I saw through this pane,' said my informant, 'an old rusty corrugated iron and a derelict shed on an abandoned site, and the thought came: "Something should be done about it; it is too depressing to look out on that, week by week." I considered asking the

11

Premises Committee, now that opaque glass is again available, to make the whole window opaque once more.

'But bit by bit, the inevitable analogy made itself felt. Perhaps not here any longer, but we know that there are places where unwanted, displaced human beings are an offence to the fastidious eye, a challenge to the Christian conscience. Many of us feel ashamed *to admit how often we are tempted to put the pane of opaque glass between us and them.* I cannot', she added, 'pray with John Wilhelm Rowntree: "Lord, lay on us the burden of the world's suffering", because I am not big enough. But I can pray: "O God, *keep clear in my heart one pane of glass*, that I may never fail to see the need, and seeing it, to find Thy way of service." '

This used to be called 'Loving' – loving one's neighbour as one's self. But the Christian word has so long been tossed about in the market-place, and in the newsagent's cheap magazines, that those of us who would glimpse its meaning are driven to look elsewhere. But Love, of course, is still alive, and in many places – *The Love of God, and human love*, that for its fullest expression depends upon God, Creator and Lover of our world. Knowledge of it comes to us most fully, through the revelation in Christ – the Incarnation – His walking earth's dusty ways, meeting people, their problems and perplexities, and through all the comings and goings, speaking of God's world, and His being within the world.

This is an extraordinary reality. We might well wonder at it – that Jesus should view His ministry as *a world ministry*, the Kingdom of God's world. 'Christianity', as Dr William Barclay rejoiced to recognize, 'is a world religion. "Go!" said Jesus to His followers, "and make disciples of all nations" (Matthew 28:19-20 A.V.). The difficulties', the Doctor continued, 'looked insuperable, and the problems looked insoluble. Amid the world empires, Palestine was a tiny country, measuring no more than a hundred and fifty miles from north to south, and fifty miles from east to west. It never had a population of more than four and a half million people. How could anything proceeding from a country like that become a world religion? Worse, the Jews were notoriously hated and despised. Cicero called the Jewish religion "a barbarous superstition", and Tacitus called the Jews "the vilest of people". Then, as now, anti-Semitism flourished. How could a religion, originating among a people hated and despised of all men, become a world religion? Further, the Jews were an exclusive people who despised the Gentiles even more than the Gentiles despised them. They were certain that they were God's chosen people, and equally certain that God had no use for any other people ... They never were characteristically a missionary people. How could Jews possibly come to feel a yearning to bring all other peoples into the Love of God?'

Into this situation, with its doubly depressing background, came Paul, a Jew, and proud of his race. Of all men, he seemed most unlikely to be a whole-hearted servant of a world kingdom. But by the mercy of Christ, he did in fact become the world kingdom's boldest and best interpreter, though cast out of many cities, beaten, shipwrecked, imprisoned. 'Of all mad things in history,' added Dr Harry Fosdick, 'can you think of anything madder, with Nero upon his throne, and Paul in his prison, than to have believed that the Gospel for which Paul stood, would outlast and wear down the empire? Who, in a sober and realistic hour, could have supposed that Paul would outwear Nero? But that was exactly what happened.'

It is a great thing, at any time, to say: '*I believe in God's world*', and to serve that belief with all one's faculties. It was no small one-donkey affair to which Paul gave his heart, but to God's Kingdom, a world Kingdom! It must at first have seemed, even to Paul's brilliant mind, almost beyond belief. Yet he came to see the whole world as

God's world, *and God sufficient in it.* Nothing – death or life, angels or principalities, or powers un-named, things present, or things to come, or height, or depth, or any other creature, would be able to separate us from the Love of God, 'which is in Christ Jesus our Lord' (Romans 8:38–9 A.V.).

And God still reigns in His world, in loving purpose. A while ago, a surprising error crept into a printing of a programme for Handel's *Messiah.* What was meant to read 'The Lord God Omnipotent reigneth', was printed as 'The Lord God Omnipotent *resigneth*'. That would be the greatest calamity in world history; but it has not happened – and will not happen. We are God's people in God's world – this world!

'The Christian Church' – confirming this – 'is now, for the first time,' as Bishop Lesslie Newbigin says, 'no longer confined to a small part of the earth, but is present – normally as a small minority – in almost all parts of the inhabited world.' Little by little, this reality is being woven into what we call 'the world Church' – ministering in many ways already to many millions. And each local congregation that knows itself part of it, knows the world challenge, and needs to summon up a response. Every time I enter St David's with that beautiful globe on its communion table, it seeks me out deeply.

And every time I recall my visit to St John's in Nelson, to lead its worship, I remember as clearly the response of one young disciple of our day. 'When you go to St John's,' said somebody to me, 'get them to show you Bill File's world.' He could see I was puzzled, but he said no more. Once inside the church, all came clear. 'Bill was a natural leader,' said his minister, whose guest I was. 'Bible Class leader, Captain of the Boys' Brigade, soloist in the choir. And he excelled at sport – cricket and tennis, hockey and indoor basketball. The Brigade selected him to represent it on the other side of the world, but he died before that

14

came off. He would have loved it. Of all the times when Bill led devotions in the Youth Assembly, I can't remember an occasion when he didn't intercede for other parts of the world. He was a world citizen, always thinking of those less fortunate, on the margin of poverty or fear.' With that we both fell silent, and moved to look more closely at the continents and islands on Bill File's memorial – an illumined globe!

It needs more of us to say, in a truly meaningful sense, 'Let me show you Bill File's world!' For it is, in reality, *God's world; and yours and mine, 'Here and Now!'*

I BELIEVE ... IN MY LORD'S DUAL NATURE

If Christianity is supremely a relationship with a Person – as I believe it is – the more we can know of Him, the better. Surely? As I make this attempt to draw closer, Martin Luther's words ring in my ears: 'Take hold of Jesus as a man, and you will discover that He is God!'

So I think of Him both human and divine – beginning first with His human nature, born in a particular time in history, in a particular place. One of my greatest moments in that little land of Palestine was in Bethlehem, that very place. I entered with a knot of friends, through the doorway of the Church of the Nativity, built over that sacred spot. Once, its doorway had been much taller, its arched height opening impressively. But straying beasts came, and infidels riding proudly; then those who cared re-made this doorway, to be low and of creamy hand-hewn stone. So that now one must enter fittingly, with bowed head; and it is something never to be forgotten, for there: *'In the fulness of Time, God sent forth His Son, made of a woman . . . to redeem.'* (Galatians 4:4f.) A very early tradition sees the birth-place as a cave; as early as the year AD 215, Origen could say to any pilgrim going that way: 'They still show the cave in Bethlehem where He was born.' Caves are still used thereabouts as stables and cellars. Nearly three and a half centuries later, the church was built over that sacred spot by Constantine. One scrambles down into the grotto today, by steps that have been provided by reverent souls; and the first thing one notices is the beautiful silver star at one's feet, bearing in Latin: 'Here Jesus Christ was born of the Virgin Mary.' Hanging oil lamps are all around.

And it is relatively easy to follow thereafter the Babe's

growth – a little refugee soon into Egypt, and back;
to grow up in a carpenter's home in Nazareth. The
hills then as today, where doubtless he ran in the
wind, with other village boys; the water supply, 'Mary's
Well', there in the village – wells never change; though
carpenter's shops and tools on the bench may. (I spent
some time quietly watching a craftsman there.) In our
day, Phyllis Hartnoll speaks of the Lad among the wood-
shavings:

> Silent at Joseph's side He stood,
> And smoothed and trimmed the shapeless wood,
> And with firm hand, assured and slow,
> Drove in each nail with measured blow.
>
> Absorbed, He planned a wooden cask,
> Nor asked for any greater task,
> Content to make, with humble tools,
> Tables and little children's stools.

Without doubt, much of His developed fitness derived from
work at the carpenter's bench. It was hard work, and He
was strong and able – not in any way frail or effeminate.
Had He been as shown often in stained-glass windows, and
holy pictures, He couldn't have done that work – which
entailed the cutting down of trees in the forest, as well as
the painstaking work on the bench. And fishermen – strong
'he-men', able to withstand storms on the lake where
they earned their living, working through the night whilst
others slept – they wouldn't have felt His appeal, and
followed Him. And they did! His eyes must have been
remarkable, dividing the true from the false at all times;
rejoicing in the simple movements of birds and flowers,
and children playing in the market-place. A memorable
moment was recorded that day when the Rich Young
Ruler 'came running' to Him: 'Jesus, looking upon Him,

loved him' (Mark 10:21 A.V.). And again later, when the Cross was no distance off: 'The Lord turned and looked upon Peter' (Luke 22:61 A.V.). What was there in that look? And there were many other occasions – beginning with Mark's first comment, in the first gospel, in point of time: 'When Jesus passed by, *He saw*' (Mark 2:14 A.V.). He kept on doing that – He saw Zacchaeus up the tree; He saw Mary Magdalene flitting from shadow to shadow in the back streets looking for love that she could never find; He saw the widow of Nain, wending her way to her son's burial, her tears falling; He saw the city, that He loved above any other city – and wept over it. Manly tears, they were, as at the burial of his good friend, Lazarus.

And His speech was the speech of a man – strong, cleanly-thought, sincere. 'Never man spake like this man,' said the crowds. Most times, they wished He could stay longer – sometimes they followed Him till their food gave out; sometimes into streets and houses so crowded that to get in a sick one they had to take off part of the roof; sometimes they stayed so close, so long, that there was not time 'so much as to eat'. There was something about Him that appealed to the sad and distraught, and the most vigorous men and women.

His name, *Jesus*, was a common name in those days, matching the fulness of His manhood. It was, in fact, the Greek form of *Joshua*. Dr William Barclay declares that: 'At least five Jewish High Priests were called Jesus, and in the works of the Jewish historian Josephus, there appear about twenty people called Jesus, ten of them contemporary with our Lord . . . *So the very name marks out Jesus from the start as a man among men.*' Early in the first gospel, in point of time, even those strongly muscled fishermen found themselves asking: '*What manner of man is this*, that even the wind and the seas obey Him?' (Mark 4:41 A.V.).

18

They were approaching the place where what they knew of His human nature began to merge with what they were to learn of His Divine nature. And as a modern disciple, I have come to that point, too. It is not enough – and never could be – to see Him only as 'a good man', even the best man of all time. 'He was made man.' But that was only half the story. He was Jesus Christ, Who being in the form of God, thought it not robbery to be equal with God (Philippians 2:6–11 A.V.). 'Wherefore God also hath highly exalted Him, and given Him a name which is above every name, that at the name of Jesus ever knee should bow, of things in heaven, and things on earth, and things under the earth, and every tongue should confess *that Jesus Christ is Lord, to the glory of God the Father.*'

'Christ' is the name we find men using when they refer to His Divinity. The name, scholars remind us, is the same word as 'Messiah'. 'Christ' is the Greek, and 'Messiah' is the Hebrew for *anointed*. Here we have to look at Him, in His relationship to God Himself – and soon we are out of our depth. God, from the very start, offered Him as His own beloved Son; and continued to honour Him as such. At His baptism, He said: 'This is My Beloved Son, hear ye Him!' And to the end it was so – till the shadow of the Cross lay over His way, and He sat talking for the last time before He and His disciples parted. 'If ye had known Me,' was the way He spoke of that special one-ness, 'ye should have known My Father also; and from henceforth ye know Him, and have seen Him' (John 14:7 A.V.). In other earth-words, 'What you have seen of Me in Time – My Spirit, My purposes – that, God is eternally.' 'Believest thou not that I am in the Father, and the Father in Me? the words that I speak unto you, I speak not of Myself: but the Father that dwelleth in Me, He doeth the works. Believe Me that I am in the Father, and the Father in Me: or else believe Me for the very works' sake' (John 14:10–11 A.V.). There

19

was something extraordinary about Him – His interest in men and women and their affairs, and His breadth of sympathy and understanding. 'He belonged to one of the narrowest of peoples, the Jews,' one scholar contends, 'but He was absolutely free from all their national prejudices and peculiarities . . . He delighted to call Himself "*The Son of Man*" and, whatever that much-discussed phrase may mean, it certainly means this among other things: that He belongs, not to any one family or race, but to all men; and, not to any one age, but to all time.'

He comes today as closely, and as challengingly, to the Indian as to the Englishman, the Austrian as to the American. He is God as well as Man, coming out of the inaccessible distances, and drawing indescribably near. He is Human and Divine. And we must keep a proper balance.

I had a strange Sunday lately. I went to my own church to worship in the morning, and as part of the Service, I was requested to stand and recite 'The Apostles' Creed'. In the afternoon, I motored a visitor to see the chapel at Selwyn Village, the Anglican settlement for old people. A strong sea-wind was blowing as we reached it. I pushed at the front door, then suddenly realized that it wasn't the wind that was the reason for it being closed: a service was at that moment going on inside, with a clergyman and choir. All eyes were turned in our direction as we entered, and we were shown in to a front seat. It was embarrassing; but next moment – the service having reached that part – we were called, with that packed congregation, to stand and repeat 'The Apostles' Creed'. The second time for me. Nor was that all.

At night, I snicked on a broadcast, for the benefit of our friend, from a far-distant Presbyterian Church, and to my surprise, I was again called to declare my faith in terms of 'The Apostles' Creed'. Three times in one day!

Thinking back over my full Sunday, I found myself

recalling Dr Lloyd Douglas's reason for writing his popular book *The Robe*, centred on the life of our Lord. 'The Apostles' Creed', he confessed, had never seemed to him satisfactory, in the way in which it moved from His birth, 'Born of the Virgin Mary . . .' straightway to His death, 'Suffered under Pontius Pilate' – *with nothing in between but a comma*. So he set out to fill in the part where the comma occurred, clothing it with rich humanity.

Scholars and preachers persist in reminding us that our faith is founded on fact, that it is a historical reality. Somewhere between the Babe's first cry, and the last uttered cry of the Man on the Cross, was a matchless life – and the Creed passed it with a comma! How could that ever be enough? He was *divine* – there was no questioning that – but He was also *human*. 'When the fulness of Time was come,' says a wonderful verse in the New Testament (Galatians 4:4–5 A.V.), 'God sent forth His Son, made of a woman . . . to redeem.' For nine months of womanly patience, He lay cradled in the womb; so human that in time He was born to be suckled; and in time, wrapped and hurried away from Herod's anger, a refugee; so human that He grew, and in the village home of a carpenter and his loved wife, learned to talk, and to walk, and, in time, to work.

The moment one skips that comma without thought, or joins the Docetists, *afraid to acknowledge His humanity, lest it distract from His divinity*, or any who suspect that He was only playing at being a man, the Incarnation has lost its meaning. Divinity and humanity do not cross out each other; the gospel portrait given us by those daily with Him, shows One undeniably human, as well as undeniably divine. Those very disciples were men, brought up to believe that God was *one God*. Yet, soaked in the Scriptures, sleeping with their Master out under the stars, often, sharing meals, growing tired as any other, knowing elation, grief, they yet believed in Him. Even before His death, they had everything to lose, it seemed, among their co-religionists — yet they held to His humanity and His divinity!

And here and now, I believe in my Lord's dual nature. If He is to be close to you and me, in this human situation in which we find ourselves, *then we have to know that He knows what life here is like!*

I BELIEVE ... IN PERSONS

Many in our midst today suffer a devaluation of money; many a devaluation of *personality*. And this is more desperate. It is easy to become a statistic in the name of progress – one of a faceless mass fed into a computer; at the hand of a clock, or a whistle-blow, urged into great offices and factories for production; spilled out later, tired, into crowded streets, controlled by lights at mass crossings – at home, to become each a digit on a census paper, to be served once a year with a tax demand pushed through the letterbox. It would never occur to any one of us to leaf through the dictionary for a definition of 'person'. And if we chanced to find it as 'an individual human being', it would be hard at times to recognize the validity of such a definition.

I used to listen to the voice of Nancy Spain, that lively spirit on the radio, and to read what she wrote in books. Suddenly, she met her death in a plane crash. That left a sorrowful gap, not only in the *My Word* team on the BBC. I shall never forget the striking tribute that Dennis Norden, one of her colleagues, paid her, finishing with the words: 'She was a person of value!'

But in the most real sense, surely, each of us is that. '*I believe . . . in persons!*' It is an essential part of my Christian faith, though I have never yet been required to rise in church, as with the Creed, to state it. But Jesus's attitude was such throughout. (I like to say that He was not a *thronging* Person – He was a *touching* Person! I have just concluded my expression of His Incarnation.)

He came into this life, touching –
a babe – reaching out tiny fingers;

23

soon, a child, amidst the shavings
of a carpenter's bench;
soon, a member of a family, a youth
bringing water from the well;
soon, earning from village customers
to pay for daily bread;
and from that time on, ministering – touching,
mindful of each person in a throng!

R.F.S.

There is no more stimulating ploy than to leaf through
the gospels. There one finds Him taking the village children on His knee (Mark 10). And that was a surprising
gesture from a religious teacher, generally expected to hold
himself aloof, to be distantly sought. Of one person the
record says: 'Jesus, moved with compassion, *put forth
His hand and touched him*' – of all men, a leper! (Luke
5:13 A.V.)

Matthew rejoiced to balance such an experience with
an equally surprising one of a woman (Matthew 9:20
A.V.): 'A woman, which was diseased with an issue of
blood twelve years,' he said, 'came behind Him, and
touched the hem of His garment; for she said within herself, "If I may but touch His garment, I shall be whole."'
(She must have been long looking at His surprising way
with other persons.) 'Jesus turned Him about, and when
He saw her, He said, "Daughter, be of good comfort; thy
faith hath made thee whole."'

Again, in Mark's gospel, we have another – one deaf,
and hindered in mixing with his fellows. But I have no
words that can tell of it clearer than how Mark sets it
down (Mark 7:31 A.V.): 'Departing from the coasts of
Tyre and Sidon, He came unto the sea of Galilee, through
the midst of the coasts of Decapolis. And they bring unto
Him one that was deaf, and had an impediment in his
speech; and they beseech Him to put His hand upon him.

24

And He . . . touched his tongue; and looking up to heaven, he sighed . . . and straightway his ears were opened, and the string of his tongue was loosed, and he spake plain.'

Towards the close of the Young Master's earthly life, Luke is provided with another incident to tell. It was in the Garden, where the soldiers came after dark, to take Him prisoner (Luke 22:50 A.V.). There was much tension. And He might – under the circumstances – have been excused care for any person other than Himself. But no! He quickly took in the distress of another. Some man present had whipped out his sword, and smitten off an ear of the servant of the High Priest. And the gospel records of Jesus in that hour: 'He touched his ear, and healed him.'

He was truly showing men and women His Father, as He said: 'He that hath seen Me hath seen the Father' (John 14:9 A.V.). And this we must know, if our life is to be meaningful. In his book, *The World and God*, written in our day, Dr H. H. Farmer's first words are: 'The conviction that *God is personal, and deals personally with men and women*, lies at the heart of Christian experience and thought . . . Only because the forgiveness of God is a transaction between persons is it able to be – as Jesus said it should be – the inspiration of a man's forgiveness of his fellows . . . This being so, it would seem that here we confront one of the main difficulties in commending the Christian faith to this age, and in maintaining it as a living power amongst those who profess it. For the modern man, seemingly, has a certain inhibition in his spirit from experiencing, and thinking of God as personal. This is doubtless the result of many co-operative causes working over several generations, such as, for example, *the increasing de-personalization of industrial relationships since the beginning of the machine age.*'

To God, persons have always mattered – not because the nicest among them have dared to believe it, or because down the centuries humanists have said so; but because God focused Himself in a Human Person, Christ. For along with Creation, the Incarnation was the greatest thing God ever did. God became Man. He still believes in persons – though some of us, it seems, don't or have grown lax about this.

My tall dear friend, the Reverend Bill Topliss, some while ago felt this loss. He stepped from a familiar English street to keep an appointment with his dentist. The moment the receptionist saw him, she raised her voice to announce: 'Here is the 10.30!' Bill confessed, on his return, his loss of personality. 'It seemed', said he, 'as if I was chuffing into Euston Station!'

Delightfully told! But this is a serious matter – a man is more than steel and steam: he is a person – body, mind and spirit. And recognizing it is one of the most Christlike points in relationship. Added to all that I have recounted of the record of His personal relationship, *the first thing He did at His resurrection, was to call Mary by her own name!* (John 20:16 A.V.).

Dr Paul Tournier – one of countless Christian doctors today – says, speaking for many besides himself: 'The proper name is the symbol of the person. If I forget my patients' names – if I say to myself: "Ah! there's that gallbladder type, or that consumptive I saw the other day", I am interesting myself more in gall-bladders and lungs than in persons. And the relationship between doctor and patient goes wrong. The personal touch is gone, and the patient ceases to be a person and becomes a bit of mechanism to be put right – and he knows it.'

Nurses, I notice, in many hospitals today are wearing neat name badges on their uniforms, to serve relationships with their patients. And many within churches are doing the same; and not only at social events associated with the congregation, can a stranger, or a shy person, speak to another. I was pleased to note lately in my own church, that when an infant was baptized during morning worship, on the Order of Service appeared both names of father and mother, and that of the little one. So that when – as part of the service, the congregation stood to take its vow of joint responsibility – it did not welcome 'somebody's' babe, but 'Peter and Gwen Thompson's little Owen John'.

What governments and their departments sometimes forget, we men and women of the Eternal Father's family must remember – for the Church in the world is a family of persons!

On the platform of Manchester Free Trade Hall at a great Mission Rally, once, I stood with George Thomas, MP – as he then was – now Speaker of the House of Commons. It was a large company we faced, and we were fellow-speakers. His words, from the start, flowed out eloquently. He emphasized the personal values of our common Lord, and our responsibility in service. He instanced the new motor roads, striding the land. He gave up-to-the-minute statistics relating to increasing speeds and road deaths; and he did more. He told of his sister. 'She was forty-two years old,' said he, 'and the mother of six children. She was knocked down from her bicycle and killed. That year nearly five hundred people died on the roads of Britain – but for me the number took on a new significance. Our Ada was one of the number; just a statistic to someone else, *but a loved one to us.*'

I was fortunate from the first – I had a good home. It was on a small farm, in Clover Road, Nelson, in New Zealand. Often money was scarce, so that we seldom bought sweets, and never biscuits – our mother made them. But we were rich in that we had extraordinary love in ordinary relationships. As we looked at our father and mother, facing long, busy days together, we came to know what it was to have *a place to reckon from*. About that time, a Scottish lad was wounded in Mesopotamia – and John Buchan, the loved story-teller of my 'teens, told of him, and of one who chanced on him as he was visiting the wounded. He asked the lad whereabouts on the battle-field it was that he got his wounds. He replied more significantly than he knew: '*It was twa miles on the Rothiemurchus side o' Bagdad!*' I like that: I understand it. The lad's home, up under the knees of the Cairngorms, was the point from which, even in that painful experience, he did his reckoning. And that, I believe, is the most important thing about a home.

It begins, of course, in the relationship of two persons – young, forward-looking. 'The rich adventure of family life begins not with things, but when two free self-conscious personalities rejoice in each other.' Vita Sackville-West is looking at this adventure well on through the years, with all the ups-and-downs that the years bring to the family, when she says: 'There is nothing more lovely in life than the union of two people whose love for one another has grown through the years, from the acorn of passion into the great rooted tree. Surviving all vicissitudes, and rich with its manifold branches, every leaf holding its own significance . . . Such love', she sums up, 'can be achieved

28

only by the practice of *mutual respect and personal liberty.*'

In a good home and family, values are accepted; lively concern is exercised; laughter is part of the very air one breathes. It is not only the place where one has a bed; and to which one can run with a skinned knee; where one can be sure of a seat at table; and something in his stocking at Christmas. *Home is a place to reckon from* – when friendships are being made, lasting values established, and faith decided on. It's something much more than a ring round the bath, and socks under the bed; even, as one has called it: 'The place where they have to take you in.'

I don't think it's easy to learn this all at once – it takes time, and some give-and-take. One of the saddest things on our horizon today is the loosening of ideals, the relaxing of home-ties, the breaking up of marriages. Nothing makes up for these – a bewildering sense of isolation and loneliness results – there is nothing to reckon from. Psychiatrists, doctors, social-workers, teachers and preachers are telling us all the time, though each falls back on his own jargon. And there is no lack of painful experience to call upon, So many of us seem to forget that we were born to belong. When we drift away gradually, or break away deliberately, we lose something precious. One of the old psalms needs to be set central in our minds, with its lovely words, that can become warning words: '*God setteth the solitary in families*' (Psalm 68:6 A.V.).

The sacred stability of the home has been in jeopardy a long time now. Few families are untouched; few haven't some experience of broken vows, infidelity, hurt. And it's all a great pity. Back in 1858, the number of divorces in Britain was twenty-four. By 1920, it had grown to three thousand; and those who knew about it tried to hush it up, they were so embarrassed. But by 1944 it had grown to nineteen thousand, and there was no hope of hushing it up. If one ceased to talk of it, there were still those relations and friends and neighbours affected. It was like a sad mildew settling on orchard blossom, beautiful and fresh, that promised a good harvest. We puckered our brows, and asked ourselves: 'What happened? Where did things go wrong?' We said foolishly, 'After a time this will be forgotten, and things go on as usual.' But they don't, and they won't. Something precious is destroyed, and the stability from which one reckoned has shifted, disappeared. Nothing can make up for it; and nothing compare with it, in terms of trust, love, growth, and the goodness of a rich family life. If there are tears – there is support; if there is laughter and fun – it is the fresher, lovelier and more lasting, for being shared.

That is one thing that brought me joy, so that my heart leapt the other morning to read of Meda McKenzie. Her picture accompanied the newspaper article, and it was good to see. Few others – if any – have been created a Member of the Most Excellent Order of the British Empire at sixteen. But then Meda, the young New Zealander, had conquered the English Channel that had proved too much for many. At fifteen, she had become the first female to swim our own country's stubborn Cook Strait, both ways.

Success, we are assured, has changed Meda very little, and in the one respect that I value most, I am glad of that. *Meda is a 'family person'*, so that when she had the chance of receiving her medal at the hand of the Queen, she declined that honour, because she wanted her parents to be with her on that proud occasion. Her family means so much to her. One indication of this known now to all the world through newspaper, radio and TV publicity given to her mastery of the English Channel, lies in the unexpected fact that towards the end of her Channel swim her brother Alex, seventeen, watching keenly, dived into the water to boost Meda's flagging spirits.

It had been a long battle – a family battle – for early in her growing up Meda had suffered a go-kart accident which injured her legs; and swimming had been then the therapy prescribed to strengthen her limbs. At that time nobody could have assessed the splendid family, as well as the personal spirit, that was to make her in time conqueror of those two mighty stretches of water. And Meda has no least doubt about the measure in which her success has been 'a family affair'.

These days it is good to have such a story in our newspapers, that carry so often news of marital collapse, grief and discouragement. Here is the underlining of corporate concern – close-linked planning, self-giving helpfulness, laughter and courage – discharging year in, year out the rich things of family life.

As early as 1958, concern for the home, as a place from which a reckoning could be made, was already concerning the Church. A Lambeth Conference discussion, centred on 'The Family in Contemporary Society', brought forth an affirmation a little unexpected then: 'The family', its report said, 'is a conservative institution with deep roots in the past, and wonderful resilience. Slowly and sometimes painfully it is adapting itself to radical changes in the wider society of which it forms a part.'

Never, in its long history, have there been so many societies, so many books, so many talks, and counselling sessions set to help young people starting out on home building. One would expect these to have a helpful effect on the undertaking. Ministers take great care to interview young folk, some weeks beforehand. No longer does the hope of all hinge on the long-repeated word 'obey' set fairly and squarely in the marriage service. Family life has more and more become 'a family affair'. Some have realized this much earlier than others. I remember hearing Dr John Foster tell of his family experience, in this connection, and in a way that raised my heart, so that I asked his permission to pass on his actual words. Said he: 'Not more than others I deserved, but God gave to me. That is

31

what I feel, looking back. What a start one got, in a home where there was much laughter and no fear, where forgiveness was always at hand; where one entered upon life as something wholesome and clean, with a standard set and a duty to be done. Religion was not terrifically talked about. It was everywhere assumed. I grew up knowing that it lay at the back of everything good in my inheritance.'

We cannot wholly blame the age, can we, that in so many places today this spirit is missing? Blessed with more things, and more opportunities than any generation before us, the ties that might be strengthened by blood relationship, sorrows and joys shared, work, leisure, fun, and mutual concern, are in many families slack, if not entirely missing. And nothing in heaven or earth makes up for this. For there are greater tests before us as a nation than even swimming Cook Strait on one side of the world, or the English Channel on the other. But one poet of our day bids us not be afraid. Says she:

> So long as there are homes to which men turn
>   At close of day;
> So long as there are homes where children are,
>   Where women stay –
> If love and loyalty and faith be found
>   Across those sills –
> A stricken nation can recover from
>   Its gravest ills.

(Anon)

I BELIEVE . . . IN THREE CONVERSIONS EACH

The word itself comes seldom to my ears now, as once it did, when I regularly occupied the family pew on Sundays. Curiously, even so, I find myself thinking of it more than was once the case. Once it offended my youthful spirit, the way people used it.

I mean 'conversion', of course, in its religious sense; for during the interval of years, it has come to my attention several times in a purely secular sense. The well-known publisher-author, Victor Gollancz, tells in his autobiography of his 'conversion' to Western Democracy – and that is quite a legitimate use of this word, though a lesser one, I think. For the Christian is converted not to an ideology, a political philosophy, or a system of ideas of any kind, but *to a Person* – and that Person is none other than Jesus Christ, Son of God, human and divine.

The word 'conversion' is used to speak of the change that comes in one's thought, will, whole being, as the beginning of one's Christian discipleship. It really represents a wonderful 'about face'; it's a pity it has been spoiled so often for so many, by so many. It stands for one's free decision to enter into a new allegiance; to live in terms of a new spiritual world; to show to others, perfectly naturally, a new life-style. Some speak of 'conversion' as of a moment – like 'Saul turned instantly to Paul'. But the more I think of that experience on the Damascus Road, and of modern people of whom I have read, and of people known to me, the less I feel sure that 'sudden conversions' are as sudden as they at first appear. Behind Paul's was his never-to-be-forgotten minding of the cloaks of those who sought to be limb-free to hurl stones at Stephen, the first Christian martyr (Acts 7:58–60 A.V.). Saul had mercilessly harassed the Christians, persecuting some, imprisoning others; but this wonderful, calm, witnessing death of Stephen's deeply affected him. Minding the contestants' garments, he looked at the happening from beginning to end. And when it was some time past, it still continued to work in his subconscious mind, preparatory to the experience on the Damascus Road, when he threw over his old way of life, to become busy comforting, encouraging and teaching the Christians.

But it doesn't greatly matter, I think, how one comes 'awake' – whether it is the thing of an instant, or like the gentle first rays of the sun through one's shutters; that is, like the life-awakening of young Timothy, brought up to just grow into the faith. All that counts, one way or the other, is that one should *be fully awake*.

I notice how this happens often in youth, and most naturally then. The modern-day Russian philosopher, Nicolai Berdyaev, tells of his conversion to Christ, Who claimed: 'I am the Way, the Truth, and the Life' (John 14:6 A.V.). The initial experience, coming between puberty and manhood, left much to be learned. 'I was shaken by the thought', said he, 'that I may not know the meaning of life, but the search for meaning gives meaning to life, and I will consecrate my life to this search for meaning.'

Without changing so much as a letter of this word that I heard so often in my 'teen years, the time comes – if in a setting in some ways remote from Berdyaev – when one must experience conversion again, and yet again. I do not mean that one should be emotionally stirred, as some I know, every time an evangelist comes to town, or every time a challenge to decision on Christian discipleship is made from the pulpit. George Ingles, in our day, puts it as clearly as it can be put, when he says, in *The Lord's Creed*, '*There are three conversions in a man's life – first to Christ, then to the Church, then back to the world.*'

34

I find this a practical and thrilling trilogy, affording immensely larger prospects than ever I dreamed of in my youth. I offered my life then to the Christ I read of in the New Testament, but I had not begun to study His full nature, or to read between the lines. Gradually, I got help from many quarters – not least, through reading. Dr Harry Fosdick offered me his *Manhood of the Master*, and Sir John Seeley, *Ecce Homo* – and from that point, I have continued ever since. So much there is to know of that triumphant and gracious Character; the *fulness* of Christ cannot be known in the brief years we have at our disposal here.

I like the way Dr John White (the Very Reverend John White, CH, DD, LLD, formerly minister of the Barony, Glasgow, and a former Moderator of the United Church of Scotland) put it, to emphasize the striking simplicity of a man of such experience and learning. He might have shared his experience in learned, abstruse, theological terms – but he didn't. What he had to say to us over the BBC was too important for that. He said simply: *'I met a Man!'* He began by assuring us that he was not over-fond of self-analysis, and after stating that religious faith was no invention of man, but some deeply installed discovery, he proceeded to move the light off himself, save only as it served his witness. There was Life and Joy and Peace in it; and he wanted it clearly seen for what it was.

'Why do I believe?' he queried. 'It came to me as it does to most in a flash, and as a result of long and serious thought. I got moral certainty in place of a defective logical proof. *I met a Man, ECCE HOMO!* He did not speak to me in abstract syllogisms; He revealed the Grace and Truth of God in flesh and blood.'

In those four telling words, the dynamic of a whole new life was summed up: 'I met a Man'. Born in a particular place and time, chosen of God, He was the image of God, born into our life on earth, with all its human affairs –

working, praying, teaching, healing, dying, rising again, triumphant over man's last enemy, Death. There was nobody like Him, God, of Majesty, Love and Mercy, in human form. Understandably, life in this world has never been the same since He came. In Him, the glorious purpose of our earth-life comes clearly into focus, and sin to its defeat! God meets us, as Dr J. S. Whale, learned theologian of our day, reminds us in unforgettable words: 'It is God Himself, personally present, and redeemingly active, Who comes to meet man in Jesus of Nazareth.' No longer is this possible upon the dusty roads of Palestine; but all that He was then in Time, and more – because He is now blessedly liberated from the limitations of a human body – *that He is now*.

It is to such a Saviour, Lord and daily Master that we each offer our whole personalities, in conversion:

> Name Him, brothers, name Him
>   With love strong as Death,
> But with awe and wonder
>   And with bated breath;
> He is God the Saviour,
>   He is Christ the Lord,
> Ever to be worshipped,
>   Trusted and adored.
>   (Hymn writer)

*

Then comes one's conversion *to the Church on earth*. To stop short of this is to stop short. And by 'the Church' one means not only a building at some known spot, up-raising its roof and stained glass windows to the sky, providing a landmark through the years. Far from it – welcoming, and beloved by many families and individual 'saints' through the years. It is more even than the believer gathered within any building; or beyond any congregational

36

gathering of them worldwide, as we speak of the Methodist Church, or the Catholic Church; nor is it limited to time, Here and Now. The Church into which one is converted is not even wholly of this earth and time we know, the *Visible Church*, but is also the *Church Triumphant*, made up of those who have lived, and have now finished their combat and witness; the *Invisible Church* includes the sainted dead; the *Church Militant* is made up of the Church now on earth. Jesus taught that a confession of faith in Himself should be the tie binding Church members. To make it possible for us to discharge a living witness to Him today, in a world-embracing dimension – beginning with those of His disciples who first went out – Christ has promised to be with us – His unseen Self – now that He is delivered from the limitations of His humanity, to be with us 'alway, even unto the end of the world' (Matthew 28:20 A.V.). In its most glorious nature, the Church is a spiritual reality, offering conversion, forgiveness, and enabling strength. Christ is in the building that we call 'the church' before ever we get to our pew, or the service of worship begins. Such an encounter depends only on our sincere, humble willingness.

*

And our third essential conversion is *back to the world*. Jesus did not pray that His followers should be lifted out of it, but kept within it. So Christian discipleship has to concern itself with social services along with worship services; the question is not whether religion and politics should mix, but how they should mix. This is God's world – and Christ's followers cannot live uninvolved. Dr Stanley Jones, the great missionary advocate and writer of our day, delighted to relate to us how at conversion his 'first impulse was to *put his arms round the world*'. In many ways it is easier to do this today than at any time – distances have diminished, information is so much more easily had from the most distant parts of man's dwelling, and

means of supporting our missionary prayer so much more
easily executed. On our lips is Samuel Wolcott's hymn:

> Christ for the world, we sing;
> The world to Christ we bring
>   With loving zeal;
> The poor, and them that mourn,
> The faint and overborne,
> Sin-sick and sorrow-worn,
>   Whom Christ doth heal.

I BELIEVE . . . IN LIFE AFTER EASTER

Easter, of course, means various things to various people. To some it is just a new hat; to others, time off from work; and to yet others, a day or two at the races. And there are all the rest of us for whom Easter has only one connotation: suffering, death, but most of all, Life! So important is it that we use, with a great deal of meaning, words that others use lightly: 'before Easter', 'Easter', and 'after Easter'. It came to me as a great surprise to find those latter words in the New Testament, prefaced by one other word: *'Intending'* (Acts 12:4 A.V.). What Herod had in mind was the Passover, since he was unfamiliar with the word 'Easter' as we know it, with its rich, enduring, enlivening meaning. Our Authorized Version of his chosen reaction to a line of events, speaks of a time of year, a parallel feast as 'after Easter'. We are told what he is *'intending after Easter'*. (This Authorized Version report is, of course, an anachronism, when it speaks of Herod's plan.)

From earliest Christian times down to the present, Easter has been celebrated by Christians with special joy. In early communities, and still in many countries of the world, it is the custom to salute each other on the morning of the Resurrection Day, with *'Christ is risen!'*

But in no sense is Easter, for us Christians today, an anachronism. We cannot be very certain how the word 'Easter' came into being. Some think we owe it to *Eostre*, a Saxon deity whose feast was celebrated in the spring, and which Christians took over and converted to the significance of the much more wonderful rising from the dead that Christ knew. Others are not so sure, and say that it is to the word *Oster*, meaning 'rising', that we owe our word. But it scarcely matters now – we know what we mean by 'Easter', and it has become wonderfully meaningful to us, hallowed by a thousand associations, not least, on one side of our world, accompanied by the breaking of spring, with a glorious release from the hard disciplines of winter that look like Death. And how lovely that rising of life is, with bulbs piercing the cold earth, daffodils in the long grass, buds fattening, hazel catkins hanging golden in the embracing sun.

'Intending after Easter' can only mean a lesser thing to Herod, with no heart's allegiance to the Risen Christ; actually, he had evil intentions, in keeping with his secret and public character. Our intentions 'after Easter' are very different – because we have by faith journeyed into the City with our Lord, welcomed by crowds, seen Him arrested, judged by men, flailed and ridiculed, made to carry a Cross of shame through the streets with their crowds, out to a barren hill of sorrow and grim death.

But that alone doesn't give us Easter – it is, beyond the tomb where His followers laid Him, the Day of Resurrection that does that! This, from the very first, quickened human hearts, and left them 'intending' something that they could never before have dreamed of 'after Easter'. The story of new Life, recorded in the book of Acts, belongs here. I like the way my friend and fellow-author, the Very Reverend Dr Ronald Selby Wright, Canongate minister and Moderator of the General Assembly, put it in *Life and Work* this last Easter. And nobody could have set down this tremendous Reality in simpler words: 'Without Easter there would have been no gospels as we know them, no Christian Church, no New Testament, no Lord's Day. It is because of Easter that we have a Gospel at all: "If Christ be not risen, then is your faith in vain." It is worthwhile to remember that the gospels were written *after the Resurrection*, and, one might say, *because of the Resurrection*.

40

'But for a Christian it is not enough to believe in the Resurrection – that the Resurrection "happened"; he must also believe that *Jesus Christ is the Resurrection*. It is not enough to believe in a past event; one must believe, too, in *a Living Person*. There can be a difference between belief in the Resurrection, and trust in a living Lord. Easter, then, is not just something that "happened"; it means *Someone Who is alive for ever more* – alive now, today, where we are now!'

Each day at the close of morning prayers, the members of Stanley Jones's Ashram, in India, respond joyfully and meaningfully when their leader says: 'The Lord is Risen!', with the words: '*He is Risen, indeed!*' It may be that knowing of this, or experiencing it there, or elsewhere, as I did in Switzerland, you face life 'intending after Easter' to establish the same custom. For it is a vital and enlivening experience, as well as a lovely Christian witness in this world that needs it so much. Something very real stirs me Easter by Easter, as I take upon my lips the Victory Song first set down in the Latin of the seventeenth century:

> The strife is o'er, the battle done;
> The victory of Life is won;
> The song of triumph has begun.
>   Alleluia!

> The powers of Death have done their worst,
> But Christ their legions hath dispersed;
> Let shouts of holy joy outburst.
>   Alleluia!

> Lord! by the stripes which wounded Thee,
> From Death's dread sting Thy servants free,
> That we may live and sing to Thee!
>   Alleluia!

41

Its reality fills me with wonder, and leaves me 'intending after Easter' never again to forget that all up through the years fellow-disciples have sung those words – and I am one with them. Being Christian is no lonely business, it is to be linked with countless others, the world round, closely bound to one living Lord.

A greater number than ever today join in the Reality those words celebrate, and in more languages the world round.

It is this glorious fact of the Resurrection in one's life 'Here and Now' that turns Sorrow-into-Joy; it can never happen at such depth, such height, otherwise. Men and women who knew of Karl Barth only as a learned continental theologian, might expect to find him a heavy-hearted man, speaking above their heads, and hearts. But he was nothing of the sort – and those privileged to visit the great and learned man in his home, constantly tell of their surprise in finding him the joyous spirit others knew him to be. A man with much laughter on his lips! With a joyful twinkle in his eyes! And it was not that he had been a favoured son of earth, not at all! This is made plain – and is a surprisingly vital witness – by way of his biography by Eberhard Busch. There is a fine photograph in it illustrative of a father's relationship with his children. It shows the great theologian making his way up a mountain in Switzerland, flanked by his two sons, Markus and Christoph. It was just after their younger brother, Matthias, had died following a climbing accident. Their father was grieved – and they knew it and were doing their best to uphold him in his dark hour. It was a wonderful relationship, and Barth was proud of his two sons. Of them, he said: 'My grown-up sons are my best comrades – which is not a gift bestowed on every father.' When both eventually became teachers of theology – Markus in the United States and Christoph in Indonesia – Barth the father in Europe comforted himself by their living relation ship. Said he: 'The sun now constantly finds at least one of our family awake and at work in the service of the most beautiful of all sciences.' Such was the strong comfort of their shared faith. I found myself last Easter, as Easter Day ended and darkness issued in my rest, thinking of a particular friend in Cardiff, Dr Kathleen Evans, on the opposite side of the world waking joyously to welcome in Easter Day; so no moment of the celebration would be without our praise! And that stirred my heart, and wakened my thankfulness. I cannot think what life would be for me, if I were unable to say: 'I believe in Life after Easter!'

It makes all the difference to death, and to life. Our Lord's words ring for me with singular joy and wonder: 'Because I live, ye shall live also' (John 14:19 A.V.). Without that assurance, how could I face the death of any dear friend, or family member, or my own sometime-coming death? The Resurrection of Jesus, my Lord, gives it another dimension altogether. It is the dimension of faith, of course. I heard Professor Charles A. Coulson, Rouse Ball Professor of Applied Mathematics in the University of Oxford, reply to one who asked if he had any proof of it, 'No, Science cannot prove it – *it cannot disprove it either.* If our Lord, Who has such tremendous insight, speaks like that, and if I have tested so many things that He said, and found them true, then that seems to me a pretty good beginning for my own belief in an after-life.' And learned though he was, lecturing to us on the nuclear age, he could yet be joyous, even as Professor Karl Barth was. For high and low, belief in the Resurrection of Christ, and all that it entails, makes all the difference in this world, because it is tied to the World Beyond.

So I remember His Death, and His glorious Rising Again, 'intending after Easter' this time to walk in the light of that Love, and the Power that will never let me go. I sing with John Greenleaf Whittier:

> I know not what the future hath
> Of marvel or surprise,
> Assured alone that Life and Death
> His mercy underlies.
>
> I know not where his islands lift
> Their fronded palms in air,
> I only know I cannot drift
> Beyond His love and care!

I BELIEVE ... IN INVESTMENTS

In the home where I grew up, we talked together about everything under the sun, and helped each other to sort things out. But there was one exception – nothing was ever said in my hearing about *investments.* I never heard the term till I was grown up, and came to live in the home of a banker.

I don't blame my parents – we grew up on a farm, at a time when everywhere money was short, and markets slack. And in my early adulthood, when I'd left my family home, a grim time of economic distress held the whole country in its coils. There was, where I lived and worked at any rate, no reason to talk of investments.

But it was in those days that I came to see, for the first time, an unguessed meaning in that banking and general business term. I chanced on a book by Naomi Jacob; and in that slender volume, which cost me but two shillings, I found her saying: 'I have never possessed much money, *but I like to look back and think how wisely I invested what I had.*' Then out tumbled a showing of rich returns. She said: 'I saw and heard Sarah Bernhardt, I listened to Ellen Terry, I saw Henry Irving play Becket. I saw Duse in *Ghosts.* I heard Paderewski, Kreisler, the Berlin Philharmonic, and the Vatican Choir. I have seen "The Last Supper", the Sistine Madonna, and the Mona Lisa, to say nothing of Monet's, Gauguin's, Van Gogh's and Renoir's pictures. I have seen the sun set on the Dolomites, the moon setting on Milan Cathedral, a string of barges going down the Elbe, the dawn at Lake Garda . . . These', she finished, 'are my investments and', with a glorious flourish, 'they have never failed to pay me dividends.'

I know what she means. And I could summon up a

comparable list, when I spent all I could muster on a world trip, by cutting hair for my friends at sixpence a time, selling from my shelves textbooks, and any books of a casual kind that I had done with, and walking tram sections to and from my Social Service Mission job in the central city. In those days, one could circle the world by ship for a modest ninety-six pounds, and live and travel using Youth Hostels for a shilling a night. But those shillings were exceedingly hard to raise, and were parted with cannily. I managed some good investments. I stood inches taller when I came back; and have added to that modest trip others since. So that now I can speak as surprisingly, and thankfully, as Naomi Jacob: 'I, too, have seen Milan Cathedral with its topping of saints; and Michelangelo's sensitive *Pieta* in Rome; Leonardo da Vinci's famed "Last Supper", fading from the eyes of future centuries; barges stringing down the Rhine – myself travelling on one of them; I, too, have stood before the Mona Lisa, and other wonders in the Louvre; I have worshipped in the Abbey on Iona; seen daily the Houses of Parliament reflected in "liquid history", which is the Thames; looked on mysterious Stonehenge; seen the Sea of Galilee, and paused in the Garden of Gethsemane. Nothing can refute these values, nor smudge them from my memory. And I have lived days in Assisi, rejoicing in the simple spirit of St Francis; and, back in London, lifted up my wonder-filled heart and eyes in Henry the Seventh's Chapel; stood quietly before Whistler's simple portrait of his Mother; listened to Beethoven's greatness presented to a hushed company. But my list is hardly begun. How rich I have become, with hours in great libraries poring over original manuscripts that will still be fashioning the minds and spirits of generations when time ends. And I have walked miles through the matchless English countryside in spring, with a modest pack on my back.'

An investment is a good investment whenever things like

this happen, stimulating one's whole personality. One becomes, that way, a more useful citizen, a nicer person to know, a friend quickened with joy and thanksgiving. And this can be a reality at home, or moving about one's own country – if in a different way, and to a different degree. It is not possible to travel all the time – or even desirable. One's own home, work, and circle of friends call for investments of their own kind, and become richly rewarding with the years.

One's own books and pictures, garden, and effort of one kind and another, count. I like the way George Lansbury chose to speak to us of his own experience. 'I have not been unsuccessful in politics,' said he, at his busy life's end, 'but if I had to do it over again, *I would invest my life in people* . . . rather than investing in programmes.'

And I know what he means. The hours and days I have spent with pencil, paper and typewriter, followed by proof-checking, is my writer's way of investing in people – for books can reach the inmost being of all ages, one by one, in all manner of situations. I know this, from the diverse letters that reach me from appreciative readers, men and women, young folk and old, in all English-speaking parts of the world; and a few from countries where my books are in translation. In spite of TV these days, and popular travel, a great many people are reading day by day, night by night. In a recent paper that comes to my mail-box, my publisher, Lady Collins, said: 'Whether people go to church or not, they still want to know why we are here in this life. What's the use of it? What ought we to be doing here? I believe that more and more people are looking beyond the materialism. Buying more washing-machines and dish-washers and so on, just isn't quite the answer for them.' They have a need that books can meet. So I think of my books, as *an investment in people*. And in these days of paperbacks, for which an author receives less monetary reward, many more copies can reach many more readers, so the investment is more widespread. I feel about my authorship much what Canon Peter Green, speaking for himself and, incidentally, for many another clergyman, feels about the Church work they are set to do. 'The time a man spends in a lads' club, or with the scouts, the time he spends on rambles with his young people of both sexes, the hours devoted to meetings of a purely social character . . . in a word, the time he spends in friendly intercourse with his people so that he gets to know them, is never wasted. The closer and more intimate the relationship into which he enters with his people, the more spiritual fruit it will yield.' It might take months, or even years – but an investment of any kind, in bank or business, takes patience. And so much more is it with our *investment in people*. The forces of evil in the world in which we all have to live these days are very real, and very complex; we can't afford to be too soon discouraged. But the issues are eternal: reaching out beyond our widest horizon. We are allied with God the Creator and Father of human spirits, in this undertaking. 'Brother Anonymous' is sometimes a very modern and wide-awake observer. In a journal that reached me lately, he wrote:

> People matter to God.
> Not just people
> who go to Church.
> All people matter to God.
> Not just those
> who live in the country.
> Not just those
> who live in towns.
> All people matter to God.
> People who are lonely.
> People who are happy.
> People who are ill.
> People who are well.

In Investments

All people need
to know God's love.
It is the Church's job
to tell them . . .
And the Church is
not just the minister.
It is you and me,
and the minister,
together, in Mission.

(Anon.)

In the church and community are scouts, guides, Brigade boys and girls looking for leaders – and what could be a better investment than in youth? There are Sunday school classes, and Youth Clubs with the possibilities of a long-time future opening out before them. To have a share in the making of that future – that, in God, is endless – is a wonderful privilege. All these investments are an experience in love: the love of God, but more than that, God's love for us. And no distance off, as a cheque can fly through the local office, are millions who are at this moment unable to read and write, and millions more who as yet have not even heard of God, the Father of us all, and His love expressed in the Living Christ. We can each do something about possibilities here in human lives.

Can anything undertaken in this world be a more exciting investment, or more rewarding?

I BELIEVE . . . IN VERBS

Scarcely a day goes by without my wrestling with words, despite my being an author of more than sixty books, and all in my own English. I sit feeling for the best words on each occasion – the simplest, most lively, most beautiful – when I am introducing a character, or telling of an event.

So I have sympathy with one like Carl Sandburg wrestling with a language not his own. English can be difficult. He reached America as a Swedish immigrant in his youth, and started earning his living early: helping in a barber's shop, presently driving a milk-wagon, later still sweating in the wheat fields. When he was needed, he enlisted as a young soldier. At last he became a distinguished poet, historian, novelist, folklorist; but when he was tackling a Preface, it was to confess: 'I am still studying verbs . . . Verbs', he added, 'cause all the trouble in the world.' They do – and not only in English. When a delegate to a decisive European conference, Averill Harriman, on being asked how his French was, had to reply: 'My French is excellent – *all except my verbs.*'

And that's the weakness of the Christian faith of many of us. Our nouns are excellent: 'Saviour', 'Redeemer', 'Shepherd', 'Friend', 'Prophet', 'Priest' and 'King' – we know them well, and sing them all in John Newton's immortal hymn. But we have trouble with our verbs!

The verb, of course, is the very sinew of speech – and of Christian living. Go through the gospels, and you will find that the words constantly on the lips of our Lord and Master were 'Come!', 'Follow!' and that simplest, but most telling of all, '*Do!*'. One of the most disquieting questions He ever put to His little band of disciples was, 'Wha *do* ye more than others?' (Matthew 5:47 A.V.). And there are other verbs that have their place in the gospels, and in living: '*Go!*', '*Resist!*'. After a talk with those who accompanied Him to the end, and would carry on after His crucifixion and resurrection, He summed up with these telling words: 'Truly, truly, I say to you, a servant is not greater than his master; nor is he who is sent, greater than he who sent him. If you know these things, blessed are you if you *do* them' (John 13:16–17 R.S.V.). Jesus was strong on verbs. 'My meat', said He (my very means of supporting life), 'is to do the will of Him that sent Me, and to finish His work' (John 4:34 A.V.).

I am not overlooking the importance of words. It is always my plan to say a good word for words – we use so many, and are so dependent on them, to communicate what we think and feel and intend. Some experts say that as many as twenty thousand are on our lips in a day. 'A thought', they say, 'is a spiritual thing, a sound is a material thing, a movement of air; but a word is a combination of the two, a thought become audible, so that it is spiritual and material at the same time. A word is a thought embodied in a material form.' One of the nicest things ever said of another, was said to Job by one of his friends: 'Your words have kept men on their feet' (Job 4:4 Moffatt). Information was there, but more important, encouragement. One receiving such would find himself able to stand up to life, and carry on. We have all had experience of this, and can never be too grateful for such words. As a people, hard-pressed, we learned this during the war days, when Winston Churchill spoke to the nation – his words kept us on our feet. We have all said what Thomas Wolfe, the young writer, said of a good editor friend of his: 'I did not give in, because he did not let me give in.' So we must never underestimate words, nor fail to speak to others we know to be in a hard place, words that will stand them up to life, and encourage them to go on. For that is a wonder that any one of us can effect.

'Jesus', Luther liked to say, 'used words that had hands and feet' – that is, a practical grip on life, a practical outcome. He knew *the worth of verbs*. When He came to tell one of His most widely-known stories, it became lastingly plain. It was about a fellow who had occasion to travel down a road familiar to both the Story-teller and His listeners: the lonely, rocky road from Jerusalem to Jericho. (I have travelled down it myself, by modern transport, and even today it is hazardous, with lots of twists and bends, ideal hiding-places for thugs and thieves. But in the day when that superb story was first told it was more notorious.) Who he was, or what his business, it was not important to tell – only that he was a human who fell among thieves, who beat him up and robbed him, then disappeared. Two men came down that way after a time, two men of fine words, a Priest and a Levite, both concerned with holy words. But they did nothing – they passed by on the other side. Then another came that way, a man travelling with his little donkey, a Samaritan, no less, and there had long existed a feud between Jews and Samaritans. At any rate he stopped, took in the situation, tended the poor fellow's wounds, pouring in oil and wine, helped him up onto his own small beast of burden, and got him to the inn, where he could be well tended, then opened his own purse to pay the fellow's dues, with a promise that more would be forthcoming, if there was need. His was a reaction that stretched out *to deeds – beyond words*. The cynic suggests that the other two travellers – the Priest and the Levite – were perhaps hurrying down to Jericho for a committee meeting of the Distressed Travellers' Aid Society. (Such a meeting, be it true, would doubtless see the spilling of many words. But that would never have satisfied our Lord, the Story-teller.)

Nor would it have satisfied Paul, His greatest interpreter. A little child, asked what he knew of St Paul, replied that 'he was a restless man always moving from one place to another, and wherever he was *he said a few words*'. Delightful! But Paul left behind him vastly more than words – he left deeds. He left new churches raised and encouraged, and, craftsman that he was, he left good tents; and in the manufacture of them, good fellowship. 'What a strenuous man was Paul,' exclaimed Dr W. B. J. Martin, 'his writings abound in such *active verbs as "strive", "fight", "run" and "do".*'

To us in this same generation, Dr William Barclay felt called to underline this need. 'It is much easier to discuss theological questions than it is to be kind and considerate at home, or efficient and diligent and honest at work.' True! It is the glory of Christianity to let its verbs activate it powerfully, and winsomely. 'Let us put our love not into words or into talk,' the New Testament sums up, 'but into deeds, and make it real' (1 John 3:18 Moffatt).

No wonder we lift our hearts when we hear, from the World Council of Churches, a report which says: 'In twelve months, we have distributed more than six thousand tons of food, clothing and medical supplies to the world's needy; established new homes for more than nineteen thousand refugees; sent one and a half million dollars in cash for emergency help to victims of floods, fires, earthquakes and famine; and provided more than six million dollars for Inter-Church and Inter-Mission Aid projects throughout the world – all this with no political or religious strings at all.'

Saints are still about – though some of us fail to recognize a saint when we see one. The haloes of light, bestowed by the Church up through the centuries, actually prove a hindrance to some of us. We need the help of a modern scholar, Dr Alan Richardson, who rejoices to remind us that 'a saint in New Testament terms, is not a perfected being, but a forgiven sinner. The New Testament word for a thing spotlessly clean is *hieros*; but *hagios* – the word translated "saint" – is anyone now offered to God, whatever his past history, or use, may have been. There were "Saints in Caesar's household".'

Those to whom Paul sent his greetings were not there and then candidates for stained glass windows (Philippians 4:22 A.V.). Other names of this Caesar were Nero Claudius; and everyone knows something of the infamy closely associated. In efforts to satisfy his secret physical desires, or to wreak vengeance on those who opposed him, he stopped at nothing. He murdered his brother Octavius, and his mother Agrippina, and in turn, after a reign of fourteen inglorious years, even then only thirty years of age, committed suicide, to escape death at the hands of his own soldiers. To be slaves in Caesar's household was an exacting situation. 'Caesar's Household', scholars tell us, was not limited to blood relations of the imperial household; though there is good reason to believe that Christianity had actually made converts among such – the term was freely used of any in government service. There was so little, if anything, in the setting conducive to vigorous Christian witness. 'The Saints in Caesar's Household' needed the grace of Christ to live in Rome as committed Christians.

And there were others to whom Paul addressed his letters: 'All that be in Rome, beloved of God, called to be saints' (Romans 1:7 A.V.). 'Unto the church of God which is in Corinth . . . called to be saints' (1 Corinthians 1:2 A.V.). 'To the saints and faithful brethren in Christ which are at Colosse' (Colossians 1:2 A.V.). One need only consider the harshness and immorality of those cities to know that those called 'saints' were in no sense poor, pale, pious creatures, with eyes up-turned to heaven, as they are all too often portrayed; set with the gibbet, thumbscrew or burning faggots, at least, retired from the sinful world's battles to fasting, self-mortification, and prayers. Many were all too familiar with these things – but showed through them splendid strength of character and faithfulness.

> Saints of Imperial Rome,
> Saints of the cloistered Middle Ages,
>   Saints of the modern home;
> Saints of the soft and sunny East,
>   Saints of the frozen seas;
> Saints of the isles that wave their palms
>   In the far Antipodes;
> Saints of the marts and busy streets,
>   Saints of the squalid lanes,
> Saints of the silent solitudes,
>   Of the prairies and the plains.
>
>   (Anon.)

This has the sense of Paul's understanding of the term, reaching to us through the ongoing centuries. Professor Herbert Butterfield, famous modern historian at Cambridge, says in his widely accepted *Christianity and History*: 'It is impossible to measure the vast difference that ordinary Christian piety has made to the last two thousand years of European history.' He goes on to describe it as 'the most moving spectacle that history affords'.

One wrote of Alice Meynell, essayist and poet of our day, whilst she was living: 'Her manner presents the image of one accustomed to walk in holy places, and keep the eye of a fresh mind on our tangled world.' Another spoke of the beloved Dr Bell, Bishop of Chichester, as seeming 'a modern saint par excellence – not retreating from the world, but accepting the world with all its twentieth-century tensions . . . of ecclesiastical issues, international relationships, and those of industry – and all the time so quietly walking with his Lord that whenever you met him, you were aware of his Lord's presence.' To these I could add 'Saint' Mildred Cable, laboriously trundling across the hazardous Gobi Desert, to share the Gospel; 'Saint' Dick Sheppard of St Martin's in the heart of London; 'Saint' Wilfred Grenfell, of Labrador's fishermen and their families of the frozen coasts; 'Saint' Howard Somervell, turning from the exhilaration of climbing Everest, to serve as doctor in a little mission hospital in India; 'Saint' Florence Allshorn, devoting her glorious energies to the founding of St Julian's for exhausted missionaries, and all who needed refreshment; 'Saint' John Baillie, in his college lecture room, and at his desk writing his books; 'Saint' Annie Vallotton, adding charming line-drawings to a modern Bible now available to us.

Dr Murdo Macdonald, of today – whom, utterly devoted, utterly humble, I might, in the same sense in which we are all 'called to be saints', call 'Saint Murdo' – says: 'It is possible that the Church today produces as many saints as she has ever done in any previous epoch of her history. They are, however, not so easily recognized, nor are they so eagerly venerated. The explanation for this new evaluation is complex, but', he adds, 'one reason is that the contemporary mind has fastened on *secular* substitutes.' In any case, saints are not, we notice, very eager about self-advertisement. But an ageless challenge still shimmers through that term, 'called to be saints'. To see God as the Great Reality; to rejoice in daily devotion of His living Will in the world, and to give themselves in service to their fellows, for His sake, and in the Spirit of Christ, is to be a modern saint. And setting, and special gifts, and world recognition have nothing to do with it. The mark of a saint is not perfection, but consecration.

And the saints can smile, believe it or not. I think of Hilda Porter, of London's needy folk, young and old; of Pauline Webb, another choice spirit I've got to know – 'a practical saint' – who has told me of one of 'Saint Hilda's' conversations. 'Just an ordinary chatty conversation' is the way she put it, of when she and the deaconess from Westminster Central Hall had been visiting an old lady living in a dingy back room in Chelsea. She said to them, 'My dears, I'm praying that the Lord will give me somewhere much nicer and cleaner to live.' 'So', said Hilda, 'we got down on our knees straight away.' 'To pray with her?' 'No,' said Hilda – 'Saint Hilda' – 'to scrub the floor, of course.' *Practical people, saints!*

This is not to forget that many in our day, besides the well known such as Bonhoeffer and Martin Luther King, have spent years in prison, in persecution, or have even laid down their lives for the Kingdom Eternal. Beside me, at this moment, is a copy of *A Flame in Barbed Wire*, by Egon Larson (just brought from the Library), which is the story of Amnesty International, starred with the names of Christians, in modern international persecution. As I read of their unbelievable courage, a line leaps to my marvelling mind, from the hymn we sing, set to its modern triumphal tune by Vaughan Williams: 'For all the Saints who from their labours rest.' And it is a line that embraces them all – of whatever church, clime, or time: '*Who Thee, by faith, before the world confessed!*' These are the saints – this is the glorious company we, in our modern age, are called to join. By far the greatest number of Christ's Saints have gone to their graves unchronicled, having lived amongst the challenges of their age, without preferential treatment.

A prayer as fresh today, as ever, is:

We offer Thee most hearty thanks for the grace and virtue made manifest in all Thy Saints, who have been chosen vessels of Thy favour, and lights of the world in their several generations.

I BELIEVE . . . IN TITUS

Mid-morning at our house we make coffee, and glance across to the far side of the street. For it's then that the post from the outside world is brought to our box.

> Purposefully down the street, the postman
>   moves,
> his arm in a great gesture of
>   giving,
> sowing gladness and grief, life and death
>   in ink,
> at each pause among the living.
>
> Countries he knows not, and cities, serve
>   him,
> though geography has little to
>   do
> with the hearts' territories, *here and*
>   *now,*
> when his morning's sowing is through.
>
> (R.F.S.)

It was Paul's letters – making up a large part of the New Testament – which introduced me to Titus; Paul wrote so warmly, and so often (Galatians 2:3 A.V.; Titus 1:4; 2 Corinthians 12:18). But it was the particular reference to a hard time that Paul and a colleague experienced, that endeared me to Titus. Of that, Paul wrote: 'When we were come into Macedonia, our flesh had no rest, but we were troubled on every side; without were fightings, within were fears. Nevertheless, God, that comforteth those that are cast down, *comforteth us by the coming of Titus*'

(2 Corinthians 7 : 5–6 A.V.). The Good News Bible renders this statement of Paul's: 'But God who encourages the downhearted, *encouraged* us with the coming of Titus.'

Commenting on that grateful word, James Smetham found himself saying: 'Providence, these days, often sends Titus by post.' And all the mid-mornings of my life witness to its truth! Few of us get far without a word of encouragement. We don't know exactly what Paul's difficulties were, but we do know what our own are. We do not easily speak about them, in detail, any more than did Paul; but we know the encouragement that comes from time to time by our own 'Titus'.

And knowing this, it is a good thing now and again to realize that there are others in like need. Outside the church where I worship is a large notice board, where a message is neatly printed by an artist friend to catch the eye of those of us who walk that way. A while back, one such message struck me: '*Somebody needs you. Have you written to them?*' It seemed to me that that board and the red letter-box handy had contrived to remind me of a long-time indebtedness – and the ongoing spirit Titus knew, that moved James Smetham to say: '*Providence, these days, often sends Titus by post.*'

I always thought I'd like to be a 'postie' in my early 'teens – but I never was. Now, I was being offered another chance – that board by the church, and that red letter-box, left me pondering whether I, too, might not learn to minister encouragement, in the spirit of Titus.

When Dr William Barclay first entered upon his service at Glasgow University, he told me, he was very junior on the staff. 'Sir Hector Hetherington', said he, 'was Principal, but months passed for a start, without my ever speaking to him by word of mouth. (But even in those days, there were more than a thousand members on the university staff.) I had my "ups-and-downs", of course. But nothing was ever known to happen to me, of joy or sorrow, than there was next morning a letter for me in Sir Hector's handwriting. You don't forget things like that!' You don't!

Such letters, to be effective in terms of 'comfort', encouragement, don't need to be couched in faultless words, written on good stationery, or to be of great length. They need only to be sincere, natural, and written in genuine consideration. Paul knew that secret; his letters never – from start to finish – aspired to be great literature. But they were the kind of letters that people, even in those days, kept, as people, on receipt of 'comfort' and encouragement, keep letters today. Dr Goodspeed, the distinguished Bible scholar, called them 'the greatest letters ever written'. He liked to say that 'they took the roofs off the early Christian meeting-places – mostly modest homes – and let us look inside'. And in so doing, they spelled 'comfort' and encouragement to us, in turn. They were meant, of course, to help friends in the faith; and to match whatever situation of rejoicing or crisis occurred within the Christian fellowship, which became, in time, the Church. Paul cared greatly for those to whom he addressed his letters, and with whom he could not himself be present. Many of them carried – and in the printed form in which we know them in the New Testament – greetings, thanks and blessings, by name, to his readers. Some were to kindly hosts and hostesses, who had helped Paul upon his way; some were to fellow believers new in the service of their Risen Lord; some to others in suffering, or age, or discouragement. Paul had to be always on the look-out for someone to take his letter – somebody he could trust, going the way that his thoughtful love winged his letter. Taken together over a long time, they now, perhaps, show some irregularities, some inconsistencies – but letters are like that, real letters. He sent others' love along with his own. 'The greetings of all the churches I am in touch with', he was happy to write on one occasion, 'come to you with this letter'

(Romans 16 : 16). Many whom Paul addressed in his letters were denied Christian fellowship, driven, some of them, into strange cities. They needed desperately the human support that letters could give.

And many today, inside and outside the Christian Church, have a like need. In that fresh, youthful book *Letters to a Friend*, by Winifred Holtby, one of the correspondents says: 'What poor stuff I send you in return for your wonderful letters.' 'That is odd,' replies her friend, 'I never thought that my letters were much, but yours come with a breath from a far country . . . *I feel I dare not do cheap or mean or selfish things when every week I feel myself before the tribunal of your lovely mind.*'

It was that way with St Paul's letters, with those who received them first. They were secret members of an underground movement, persecuted, often dispirited, needing encouragement – moving often down little dark back streets to the places of meeting. But what excitement was theirs when a letter came from Paul!

Today, a letter we have taken time to write can cross continents and seas, conveying affection and encouragement. The mere sight of a familiar handwriting on an envelope is often enough to lift a receiver's spirit. The more natural the contents, the more personal, the more eagerly shared, the better. Speaking of letter writing, Katherine Mansfield, of the little country that is 'home' to me, says: 'It really is a heavenly gift to be able to put yourself, jessamine, summer grass, a kingfisher, a poet, a pony, an excursion, and new sponge-bag and bedroom-slippers, into an envelope!'

Business letters are another matter altogether – dictated, self-consciously phrased, typed, or handwritten in one's best: 'Dear Sir', or 'Dear Madam'. There is no escaping such in an orderly life; but it is of the more personal kind of letter that I grow enthusiastic. It is true that people like us did once have more time. But that excuse that sends us to the telephone, or to the telegram-counter in the post office, leaves us conscience-stricken when we chance to think of certain people, and realize we haven't sent them so much as a dozen lines in as many months. It's easy to say: 'Oh, forgive me, is it that long? I did mean to send a line some time, but it somehow slipped my memory.' Paul, a model letter-writer, in his human relationships, nurtured at the cost of much unselfishness, wrote: *'I want to be among you, to be myself encouraged by your faith, as well as you by mine'* (Romans 1:11f.).

And the best way he knew of doing that just then was by writing a letter.

I BELIEVE ... IN ENTHUSIASM

I shall never forget a morning when a tall straggly currant bush in a hedge was sweet with pink flowers, and every bird jubilant. These made it particularly difficult to believe my eyes when I read an old gentleman's epitaph. It described him as being: 'Vicar of this parish for forty years, *without ever showing the least sign of enthusiasm.*' Happily, the thought then rose within my memory that I had somewhere read that the word 'enthusiasm' had changed its meaning with time. Instead of being the good, lively thing that it now is, it was then a kind of frenzy, or fanaticism. So what this epitaph was saying was that the old Vicar had been a steady character, splendidly in control of himself, and the things he was responsible for, for forty years. Today, anyone lacking enthusiasm is counted a half-alive person, and one to be avoided if possible. Someone has defined enthusiasm as 'Everything that boils over, and runs down the side of the pot'. I understand that better after reading lately Sir Francis Chichester's book *The Romantic Challenge*. He begins it with the words: 'I love life; this great, exciting, absorbing, intriguing, puzzling, adventurous life!' I had read other words from that gallant modern man of the seas; and I have an ear at any time for anyone who can begin a book with such words!

When I first began to think deeply of things Christian, it surprised me greatly to find the author of *Ecce Homo*, J. R. Seeley, saying: 'No soul is pure that is not passionate, no virtue is safe that is not enthusiastic.' He was speaking of Jesus, our Lord. But my whole personality soon rose to accept his saying as reality. And soon I came upon Dr Paterson Smyth's book, *A People's Life of Christ*, saying much the same. Till then, I must confess, I'd thought of Jesus as the Great Teacher, the Friend of the lonely and distressed, the Man of Sorrows, the Saviour of the World, Founder of the Church – but never as the Superb Enthusiast. But the more I thought about it, the more it became clear to me that he was right. 'Consider', said Seeley, 'the passion that moved Him – the great central enthusiasm. What was it? Think . . . It was the subject of His very *first* sermon. His *last* instructions in the days after the Resurrection pertained to it. The twelve apostles were sent out to teach it . . . He called this ideal of His, "The Kingdom of God".'

Many an artist, or stained glass craftsman, or hymn-writer up through the centuries, has bypassed this, and depicted Him as a pale and spiritless individual. But He wasn't, of course, a scrap like that. We have only to read between the lines of the New Testament. Apathy was clearly one thing that He could neither accept in Himself nor in others called to discipleship. He talked figuratively about 'cutting off one's right hand', if it hindered whole-heartedness – 'all other faults and deficiencies He could tolerate, *but He could have neither part nor lot with men destitute of enthusiasm.*' It is later a no less essential quality with His chief missionary disciple, Paul. The time came when, looking back, he could say, as reported by Dr Moffatt in his version of the New Testament: '*Wherever I go, thank God, He makes my life a constant pageant of triumph in Christ!*' (2 Corinthians 2:14 Moffatt).

And many another since has shown, in wholehearted allegiance, that same glorious quality, answering as eagerly as did once the Rich Young Ruler. It is recorded of him that 'when Jesus was gone forth into the way, *there came one running*' – as enthusiastic as that! (Mark 10:17–22 A.V.). He kneeled to the Master, there and then in the roadway – but it never came to anything. We never hear of him again – it was all an emotion of a moment.

Dr Paterson Smyth likes to recall some of the enthusiasts

known to him, and loved by him – there was so much in their response. 'They were men,' said he, 'eager about Missions, about Temperance, about Housing of the Poor, about Play-grounds for city children, about Old Age pensions. I had one friend who was so excited about the helpless classes in his city, and specially slum children, that every talk with him was bound to end in passionate words about them. He was a plain, humble man, but so persistently did he keep on about his ideals that he actually forced the head of a set of us in the city to found a valuable Social Service Union. Truly, this world would be a poor world if you took those enthusiasts out of it.' (Not all, of course, are followers of our Lord and Master – but a good many are.)

In the same spirit, I like to recall a number of my friends up and down this land, who have accomplished wonders. (Of course, enthusiasts are not always easy to work alongside, at home, in the church, the choir, the club, wherever one finds them active. They show up the casuals, the half-hearted, they make demands on those about them, if only by example, with no words spoken. But has any good cause ever started, much less established itself, to the glory of God among men, and the help and refreshment of the rest of us, without the enthusiast?)

I think of but one, this moment, and I know an uplift of heart. A blue-sky morning was all about me, as the phone rang, and news of the death of my Irish friend, Emmie, reached me. It was our mutual friend, my minister, the Reverend Ashleigh Petch, speaking. Emmie's death was unexpected. She was not old – and never would be, as Thoreau counted age. 'None', said he, 'are so old as those who have outlived their enthusiasms.' That is one thing that Emmie never did.

She had elected to travel from her beloved Dublin and

as a young wife, bring Desmond, her sick husband, to this side of the world, during the hazards of war, in an effort to give him a renewed chance of recovery in our rare southern air. They arrived safely, despite enemy submarine action and other hindrances; and life was the richer for many of us because of it. War slipped into the background, and the days came nearer to normal for Desmond and Emmie. After a goodly span of years, Emmie found herself bereft. I took part in Desmond's funeral service, and later memorial service; and we made a tape to send to Dublin to his aged mother and relations. Later still, I dedicated my new illustrated book *A Show of Hands*, with the words: 'Remembering my friend Desmond Smith, of strong gentle hands, and strong gentle heart.'

Emmie, with her many gifts, gloriously served through the following years, in hospitality, public speaking, music, and a wide-spread travelling appointment with the Bible Society. And now she had gone.

Ashleigh asked over the phone whether there was anything I would like him to add to his tribute at the coming service. I said, 'Yes . . . one thing that more than all, to me, sums up Emmie. When she was staying with us, up at "West Hills" once, we three were standing in the kitchen, talking of God's Kingdom, as we washed up. Suddenly Emmie straightened to her full height, and asked: *"Do you ever feel you want to sing all four parts at once?"*'

That was Emmie! She was a fine musician; but above all, she was an enthusiastic Christian. She worshipped and served utterly, and joyously. When Haydn, the great composer, was asked how it was that his church music was so cheerful, he replied, as Emmie might have done: 'I cannot make it otherwise. When I think of God, my heart is so full of joy that the notes dance and leap from my pen.'

Our Lord would understand that. You remember when somebody among the Pharisees suggested that He should check those enthusiasts who tore down palm-branches to wave, and flung their outer garments on the way, as He rode into the City of Jerusalem, on a borrowed donkey. His answer was unforgettable: 'I tell you that if these should hold their peace, the stones would immediately cry out' (Luke 19:40 A.V.).

Emmie belonged to His Blessed Company of Enthusiasts. And what a tonic such fellow humans are – and challenge. Carl Sandburg, the American poet, rejoiced in it, when he saw and heard it in a Jew fish-crier down on Maxwell Street. Unlike Emmie, who had a musical Irish tongue, he had a voice Sandburg described as 'like a north wind blowing over corn stubble in January'. 'He dangles herrings before prospective customers,' says Sandburg, 'evincing a joy identical with that of Pavlova dancing. His face is that of a man terribly glad that God made fish and customers to whom he might call his wares from a push-cart.'

But there was something more in Emmie's enthusiasm, lacking in the ever-so-laudable performance of the fish-seller – it was Christian, it was deeply thoughtful, it was an expression of utter devotion. It was of the nature of enthusiasm evinced by the early Christians, according to the scholars, speaking authoritatively of that time. It was sometimes a costly business, in terms of self-giving – but utterly sure and joyous, as a whole. It was an ongoing reality, practical in its eventual outcome; it had a glorious record of achievement. It was all and more, what the modern writer Pamela Hansford Johnson said of Joyce Carey, a fine fellow novelist: 'He saw everything twice as large, and nine times as lovely as other people.'

Our world has need of such – so it is a loss in our lives that Emmie has gone upon her way. We all need enthusiasts, as our Lord clearly inferred when asked to check those who welcomed Him into the City. We cannot get far with a casual or apathetic religion, however clever-sounding – a contradiction in itself. The great thing, surely, is to devote oneself to life, in some chosen manifestation of its glorious, rewarding self, to the very end. Thoreau, I believe, was very near a great general truth, when he said: *'None are so old as those who have outlived enthusiasm!'*

Faith, Hope and Love! The New Testament ties all three together very beautifully. But here it might be helpful to look at each in turn, and to begin with Faith (1 Corinthians 13:13 R.S.V.).

When most of us speak of Faith, we start with its reasonableness, when we should start with its inevitability. For we cannot step into a bus, marry, sow seeds in the soil, engage in business, rear children, or set out on any kind of adventure without it. If it were possible to do so, we might regard it as some kind of intellectual interest and that's all. But it is so much more than that. In this challenging world in which we live, the New Testament goes so far as to speak of 'The victory that overcometh the world, even our faith' (1 John 5:4 A.V.).

This we know to be the truth; and have found it confirmed again and again in close conversation with friends speaking trustingly; and in autobiographies and biographies read. And the Church has underlined it for us in a religious sense – though the word itself is not always used in that one way precisely. None of us, it is certain, can live fully without faith. It not only carries forward wealth from the past, it gives significance to the present, and hope for the future. All our relationships, living dreams, and undertakings need it. Faith is a prime requisite. The poet shows his down-to-earth experience when he sings:

> Think not the faith by which the just shall live
> Is a dead creed, a map correct of heaven,
> Far less a feeling, fond and fugitive,
> A thoughtless gift, withdrawn as soon as given.

In All Three

It is an affirmation and an act
That bids eternal truth be present fact.

(Coleridge)

It abides at the heart of everyday comings and goings, and shows itself in many ways. How many of the gadgets that science and technology have given us could we use without faith? – few, if any. Our life would soon come to a standstill. We pick up the telephone a dozen times a day, in the full faith that it will enable us to communicate with somebody, though all the time unseen as we talk; we listen to the radio, selectively, satisfied that we are spending our time wisely, and music blesses our faith; we come home in the evening, and put a hand to the switch just inside the door, and the electric light goes on. We do not fully understand how these ordinary essentials work – we accept them in faith. Science, in a score of other manifestations, illustrates the same. Dr J. S. Stewart says of his university friends in the ongoing service of science: 'They are continually betting their lives on two things – the rationality of the universe they are investigating, and the reliability of the mental processes they are using. *What is that but faith?* Indeed, the only way for any of us to stop using faith would be to stop living. When we lie down to sleep at night, when we rise in the morning, when we go on a journey, or make friends, or plan our work for tomorrow or next year, it's all belief in action. Take it as you like,' Dr Stewart adds up, 'faith fills every horizon and fashions every philosophy.' It's a glorious everyday fact; as Professor Kirsopp Young points out, *'Faith is not belief in spite of evidence, it is life in scorn of consequences.'*

It sends some of us to climb mountains; and some of us to open hospitals in the jungle; it sends others of us to drain marshlands; and others of us to jump out of the sky. One is never too young, or too old. Stephanie Walls, at twenty, made a perfect landing by parachute, the other day, at the North Shore Aerodrome not far from my home. A leap of 3200 feet – despite all that one might know – required faith. It was Stephanie's one-hundred-and-twenty-second jump, and she made a beautiful stand-up landing. (This kind of thing must have taken a great deal of faith at the start – not to mention what it must have meant for the very first parachutist to try such a landing. His attempt was made from a balloon, and he had the misfortune to break a leg. But even that did not end his faith in the possibility of such a jump succeeding. Within four years from that date, it was perfectly achieved, on 22 October 1797 – since which time countless men and women have landed safely, especially in wartime.)

Faith – however we think of it, even in its religious sense – is scarcely a thing of a moment; rather is it an attitude to life and its many challenges. It calls for absolute readiness, like Stephanie's, to commit one's body, mind, and total faculties – but not to a thing of man's making, in material terms, a parachute; or even to a shining philosophy; *but to a Person!* And this Person, in this greatest realm of all, is none other than the Son of God. (I wonder how much that distraught father who, long ago, sought the aid of Jesus for his sick lad, knew of Him? Certainly, he hadn't nineteen centuries to support his venture in experience, as you and I have at this stage of Christian belief; nor had he any New Testament record by way of encouragement. One can't even know how long his own brief experience was, but we remember his words: 'Lord, I believe: help Thou mine unbelief', or as Dr William Barclay translated the original Greek: 'Immediately the father cried out: *"I have faith. Help me if I haven't enough!"* ') How often our hearts have echoed those very words! For we can't make any advance without Faith.

Our Faith, of course, turns not on occasional good fortune, but upon the lasting character of Christ!

We haven't in any way need to feel 'specially religious',

when we act in faith – some tingling of the nerves, some thrill. Faith is an altogether natural essential. As one old house-help said: 'The trouble with life is, that it is so daily.' The New Testament scribe who gave us the book of Hebrews, wrote eagerly: 'Let us hold fast the profession of our faith without wavering' – and then added the basis of belief: '*for He is faithful Who promised*' (Hebrews 10:23 A.V.). Faith depends on a human measure of acceptance, and devotion; but most of all, upon the dependable character of God, in Christ. It is less our power to hold on to Him, than our readiness to allow Him to hold on to us!

There is no least need for me to look back over my shoulder when the Age of Faith is mentioned, as if it were all in the past – the Age of Faith is *here and now*!

I BELIEVE ... IN HOPE

'And where were you born?' asked my new acquaintance, as we sat side by side in a front seat of a bus going through the country. 'In Hope,' I replied. 'Is that a place?' was her next question, 'I thought it was a state.' 'It is both,' I was able to reply; for I had only that week handled my birth certificate, which year in, year out, stays in my Safe Deposit envelope at the bank. In answer to place of birth, it said simply: 'Hope.' It's a pleasant pastoral part of Nelson, and there on a clover farm, with its little tracks, and bees beneath a blue sky, I was born. I should say 'we' were born, because I have a twin sister. About ten years of age, when puzzles and jokes fascinated us, we used to say to each other: 'We'll never die in despair – because we were born in Hope.'

I doubt whether my birth-place had actually any bearing on the reality, but I think I can rightly claim that I've always been a hopeful person, from childhood up. And the more I think about it now, the more I can say: '*I believe in Hope!*' And the kind of Hope I am speaking of is something more than the kind of attitude Thomas Hardy credited to the thrush, when he broke into ecstatic song on a branch above his head towards twilight. He wrote of it, very charmingly:

> I could but think there trembled
>   through
> His happy goodnight air
> Some blessed hope of which he knew
>   and I was unaware.

It's more than that – something beyond the capacity of a

bird. It has to do with a human personality, blessed with mind and spirit, and rare sensibility. It moves even beyond a make-believe world – where some humans spend a lot of their time – into a real world. Hope is part of a clear, healthy mind, and a lively constructive spirit. 'Hope of all passions', said Young, in his widely-known *Night Thoughts*, 'most befriends us here.' And he wasn't thinking and speaking of spring, or even necessarily in spring. Though there is no overlooking the Hope that abides in spring. Forbes Robinson wrote to a friend, once, much as you and I have done time and time again: 'We are having lovely weather. The buds "feeling" after each other – new life and resurrection life – a type, a pledge of fuller resurrection, of Easter life – nay, the same life – "I am the Resurrection and the Life" – working in trees and flowers and men. What a glorious thing', he added, 'to live in a world which has been united to its Maker!'

God's world, when one comes to think of it, is conceived in Hope. Dawn follows darkness, spring follows on the leaf-strewn way of winter, the world is born anew in every little child, the Resurrection lies just beyond what we call Death.

The Christian – whether he is a gardener poring over his seed packets in wintertime, waiting with Hope for the re-birth of Nature; a parent with his gentle, secretive hope for the years as his little one's birthdays unfold; or a family member of one whose earthly days are drawing to a close, with the release that Death brings – I cannot see any real Hope for the future, except in God. Even when the Christian is struggling through some awkward or painful situation, he preserves deeply within him a zone of Hope.

I once by chance called on my old friend Mrs Evans – a great gardener, and a splendid Christian. And it was winter. I was sorry about that. 'A pity you've had to come at this time,' said she, 'when my garden is bare.' But it was her next words which sent me away with a posy of thoughts: *'Oh, if only I could show you the lilies that lie under the soil!'* That's Hope! And there is nothing sentimental or unrealistic about it – it is founded on God. Paul's words to his friends, going through a 'winter of the spirit', were about God – neither at His wits' end, nor His work's end. 'Now the God of Hope', he wrote, 'fill you with all joy and peace in believing, that ye may abound in Hope' (Romans 15:13 A.V.). Paul was in no sense a superficial character, a lightsome optimist: life was real, and life was earnest for him. But at its heart was Hope – Hope in God. He was not one to overlook his own human frailty, or that of his fellows. He knew they needed Hope, and it was not just a future expectation; it was based on actual, present experience. They could 'rejoice in Hope', because it was already in point of being realized; it was tied in with God's Will in the world, and those dedicated to the doing of it. It was a living, ongoing reality – not a vague, pleasant wish for the best.

And is this still true? Yes, it is – *'I believe in Hope.'* And I find myself strengthened by a current word from the noted Christian scholar Dr Rupert Davies, speaking against the 'doomsters'. But he is not lightly saying that things today can't be as 'wintry' as they say – he admits that he can 'see no Hope for the future except in God'. In God, he can see *clear Hope* for the present and the future for this world as it unfolds, and for what awaits us, after life here. 'The human race, or large parts of it,' he says, 'has been brought several times to our knowledge, to the very brink of self-destruction by the folly and selfishness of man – as at the collapse of ordered government when the Roman Empire broke up, by the Thirty Years' War, by the First and Second World Wars, and by the threat to use the hydrogen bomb – but it has never *quite* toppled over. We are, somehow, still alive today. Some people ascribe this to the direct act of God, some to the efforts of enlightened men. Christians ascribe it to both: to God working in and with men. Therefore always there is Hope, Hope based on God's actions in the past – and chiefly His liberating act in Christ – but also on His continued action in human affairs by the power of the Holy Spirit.'

Certainly, we cannot live in the kind of world in which we find ourselves today, without Hope in God. Nor does it end here in family and community life, and in the glorious new discoveries science is making for us, and in the struggles between the nations. Beyond this swift human life we are encouraged to look out with Hope! 'Hope' of this kind, someone has said, 'is the dream of someone fully awake!' We cannot say of Death, that 'it will not happen to us' – we know it will, however boldly we say that we 'don't want it to happen yet'.

Christian Hope at this juncture is as different from fear, or wishful thinking, as it well can be – one is not faced with 'the horror of Death', so much as 'the Hope of Life'! Every Easter Day reminds us that Christ did more than survive Death – *He conquered Death!* He never, at any time of which we have a record, argued about the possibility of Life beyond Death – He accepted it as fact, saying: 'If it were not so, I would have told you . . .' (John 14:2 A.V.). Again, He said: 'Because I live, ye shall live also . . .' (John 14:19 A.V.). And again: 'Fear not them that are able to kill the body, but are not able to kill the soul' (Matthew 10:28 A.V.). It isn't very much to say; but coming from Him, I believe it is all we need to know. A close reading of the New Testament does suggest some realities – that it will be a liberating experience. Here we are all of us subject to local and earthbound limitations. We shall then be each of us delivered from material conditions – from hurts and wearinesses, and ignorances that we find in this life very real. Our daily struggles and temptations, and bereavements, and sorrows will be at an end too. One of the nicest verses in the New Testament, looking ahead, says: 'His servants shall serve Him!' I like that (Revelation 22:3 A.V.). It ties in with what I have learned from Jesus, about making full and joyous use of given talents, choice powers developed here on earth, sometimes at great cost; I believe they will not be wasted. If Love is the beginning and end of human values, Here and There – as I believe it is, by every reckoning – then Paul's summing up is the forefront of my cause for thanksgiving: '*Now* I know in part; *but then* I shall know as also I am known' (1 Corinthians 13:12 A.V.).

Believing, as I do, in God's gift of Life, conceived, and wrought to glorious achievement for each of us in the great Future, it does not surprise me to have Captain Scott write of his Christian companion, Dr Edward Wilson, as Death caught up with them in those snowy spaces: 'His eyes have a comfortable blue look of Hope . . . peaceful with the satisfaction of his faith in regarding himself as part of the scheme of the Almighty!' That's the secret!

We men and women – wherever we live this hour, in this world today – stand in urgent need of a recovery of Hope as an ingredient in our human wholeness.

I believe, with countless others, in the words of Rupert Brooke that one day beyond the experience of Death, we shall:

> Spend in pure converse our Eternal day;
>   Think each to each, immediately wise;
> Learn all we lacked before; hear, know and say
>   What this tumultuous body now denies;
> And feel, who have laid our groping hands away,
>   And see, no longer blinded by our eyes.

I BELIEVE . . . IN LOVE

One of our best-known and longest-cherished passages in the New Testament came to us first in the beautiful Authorized Version of 1 Corinthians 13, learned by heart as children. But we couldn't possibly have fully known its meaning then, even if we do now. For its glorious depth and breadth covers the whole of our human experience here. Now, I find the Moffatt rendering of those early memorized words even more telling – and, it seems to me, worth possessing that translation for this passage alone. It seems crisper and closer to life; and the word 'love' reaches one more nearly than the Authorized's word 'charity'. This has come to carry a meaning of social welfare, these days. But even the more understandable word 'love' has, by much careless usage, lost a great deal of its loveliness. These days, filmgoers, and readers of cheap magazines and paperbacks, are often nauseated by the use of the word, as we come upon it in our family life, school life, work and play, not to make any exception of our religious life. The word has been stripped of its content, to be clothed only in base desires, sentimentality, fleeting passion, or glamour. It is used in relationship of one man and one woman. Though it can reach heights there, if properly understood and used – as Elizabeth Barrett Browning and her Robert show us in one of the choicest love poems in our language. Elizabeth's words never lose their lustre:

How do I love thee? Let me count the ways.
I love thee to the depth and breadth and height
My soul can reach, when feeling out of sight
For the ends of Being and ideal Grace.

I love thee to the level of every day's
Most quiet need, by sun and candle-light.
I love thee freely, as men strive for Right;
I love thee purely, as they turn from Praise.
I love thee with the passion put to use
In my old griefs, and with my childhood's faith.
I love thee with a love I seemed to lose
With my lost saints – I love thee with the breath,
Smiles, tears, of all my life! – and if God choose,
I shall but love thee better after death.

But the Love of which the thirteenth chapter of 1 Corinthians speaks has a dimension even greater – the pity is that we have only one word on our tongues most of the time, for many kinds of love. The Greeks had many words – *eros*, for love of beauty, fired with passion and laden with desire; *philia*, the unselfish, steady feeling of a man for his friend; *philadelphia*, used only of actual kinship; *philanthropia*, expressive of a kindly general attitude towards mankind. Then there was the great Christian word *agape*. One has only to compare the *agape* of the glorious passage Paul gave to the world, reflecting the spirit of Christ, to appreciate that an impassable gulf yawns between them. *Agape* is not found in any of the non-Christian writers – it is a word, wonderfully rich with meaning, born within the bosom of Faith. It reaches up to God – and out to one's fellows. It is pure, clean and strong, and never fails – it lasts. It does not necessarily change any situation – but it changes relationships. Many a neighbourly link, friendship, or marriage has died for want of this Christ-like Spirit.

No one in our day better knew the importance of Love, in its truest, best sense, than did Florence Allshorn, that choice soul who founded 'St Julian's' in one of England's quiet places, to receive returned missionaries, and others desperately in need of refreshment. And as she faced the responsibilities of St Julian's, she knew well how much she needed that redeeming power herself. Amidst the multitudinous claims on her, she made room for a quiet time of devotion wherein she could read that whole chapter on Love, every day, for a year! (1 Corinthians 13 : 1–13, finishing with the first verse of the next chapter, beginning: '*Make Love your aim*'. Moffatt translation.)

During that time, she wrote of her experience, and its outreach, in a very beautiful, honest way, that we might all be helped into this essential Christian secret : '*Life became an adventure in learning to love* . . . I used to think that there was something in me that was too precious to run the risk of mixing with ugly, ordinary things – a kind of mystical dream that might grow into something very beautiful, if I kept my mind up in the clouds enough and did not allow it to be soiled. I can't explain it, but it was purely selfish. And now I know that life is clean, dirty, ugly, beautiful, wonderful, sordid – and, above all, Love. I even used to think', she confessed, 'that I was rather good at that. I used to think that being nice to people, and feeling nice, was loving people. But it isn't, it isn't. *Love is the most immense unselfishness, and it's so big. I've never touched it.*'

Whether we can summon what it takes to keep up a daily reading of this glorious passage on Love that Paul gives us in 1 Corinthians, I know not. From the twenty-seventh verse of the previous chapter, we are made aware of the day-to-day setting in which Love is to be a living reality. 'Now', it says, 'you are Christ's Body, and severally members of it. That is to say, God has set people within the Church to be first of all apostles, secondly prophets, thirdly teachers, then workers of miracles, then healers, administrators, and speakers in "tongues" of various kinds . . . And yet I will go on to show you a still higher path.' (And this is the path of Love, in its most winsome, but practical, way, among our fellows.) Thus

I may speak with the tongues of men and of angels
but if I have no love,
    I am a noisy gong or a clanging cymbal;
I may prophesy, fathom all mysteries and secret lore,
I may have such absolute faith that I can move hills
    from their place,
but if I have no love,
    I count for nothing;
I may distribute all I possess in charity,
I may give up my body to be burnt,
but if I have no love,
    I make nothing of it.

'Love is very patient, very kind. Love knows no jealousy;
love makes no parade, gives itself no airs, is never rude,
never selfish, never irritated, never resentful; Love is never
glad when others go wrong; Love is gladdened by goodness, always slow to expose, always eager to believe the
best, always hopeful, always patient. Love never dis-
appears. As for prophesying, it will be superseded; as for
"tongues", they will cease; as for knowledge, it will be
superseded. For we only know bit by bit, and we only
prophesy bit by bit; but when the perfect comes, the
imperfect will be superseded. When I was a child, I talked
like a child, I thought like a child,' said Paul, 'I argued like
a child; now that I am a man, I am done with childish
ways.

At present we only see the baffling reflections in a
    mirror,
    but then it will be face to face;
at present I am learning bit by bit,
    but then I shall understand, as all along I have
myself been understood.

Thus faith and hope and love last on, these three, but th

greatest of all is Love. Make Love your aim . . .'

Little wonder that Florence Allshorn felt that 'Love is so big!' And yet it is so minute, and tender. In the most unfortunate and confusing situations that our world throws up, it shows itself – and always it is adequate. A long-time friend was guest in our home at the end of the war, and she told us of an experience of Love that showed itself in a grim prisoner-of-war camp where she had been. I've never forgotten it – and never shall. Leila had been serving with the YWCA when suddenly she was taken prisoner. (For a time, we had had no news of her, but when at last she appeared, and returned home, she told us how it was.) When the Japanese occupied Java, the majority of Dutch men were imprisoned within a few weeks. It was only months later that arrangements were made for the internment of the women and children.

'In the camp in Batavia where I was,' said our friend, quietly, 'was a young Dutch woman whose first baby had been born after the father had been imprisoned. The little girl was lovely, and quite naturally, the mother longed for her husband to have the joy of seeing her.

'For some months she was at a loss to know how it could be achieved; then her love triumphed. The birthday of the young husband approached; and after much thought, she made a request to the Japanese authority for permission to take the child to the barbed wire of the prison where her husband was held, and to send her in to greet him on his birthday.

'There was great jubilation when the Japanese gave consent for the mother to take the baby. Friends in the camp heard the news, and in time – having offered little gifts out of their poverty, to help the baby look nice – saw her set off. It involved a walk of some distance to the agreed barrier. She herself was not allowed to see her husband,' said our friend, 'but with the courage of love, trusting in the innate gentleness towards children characteristic of the Japanese, she handed over her baby to the Japanese guard, who took her to her overjoyed father. Meanwhile, the long minutes ticked by. *Later, the guard brought the little one safely back to her waiting mother.'*

Amazing love! There was something God-like about it — for God loves utterly. As men and women often we find it hard to do that — and we love some about us, some of the time, but not all about us, all of the time.

Love goes on to show itself in loving others as they are, not waiting until they have improved, and are somewhat like we could wish them to be. Again, Love doesn't ask to check others' qualifications before being ready to offer Love. Love is the God-like power that disregards these matters, and gathers into full life many odd points of living.'

Lately, I have spent a good deal of time rethinking the way I have myself travelled in life till now, and the following poem is the comment that comes to the fore:

A first teacher is remembered long,
An early lark remains a sightless song,
Manhood breaks a boy's flute for speech made new,
Four living seasons nudge us the year through,
Whilst finer than woods foliate in May,
Friendship makes beautiful one's common way,
And Love, trusted truly, shows itself a power
Enough for the challenge of any hour.

(R.F.S.)

I had been in and out of London that year, more times than I can now remember. But this particular time held an experience I shall never forget. On a day marked some time earlier in my little red appointment book, I made my way to Chelsea Old Church. I had never been there before, nor have I been there since.

That day, the old Thames ran by, as ever – no tame piece of water, but rippling, recalling the saying shared by an old waterman, who declared that centuries earlier 'a set of fiddles had been drowned in the Reach, and the River had been dancing ever since'.

But I soon forgot the river, in the peace inside the Old Church. It had been bombed on a fateful night during London's bombing, and later repaired. But despite this so recent grief, it was beautiful – and in that hour out of time, filled with a reverent weekday congregation. On the altar, my eyes fell instantly upon the eternal symbol, the Cross; and beyond it, just outside a gracious window, a great tree was filigreed against the sky. It was satisfying to the spirit, in that holy quietness.

But that was not to miss a unique feature of the Old Church: a goodly number of embroidered kneelers beneath the pews. In chaste colours they commemorated parishioners of a long past time – back to Sir Thomas More, no less, and his family circle and friends. And his servants were included, chief of them Dorothy Colley. In a letter, her master in those grim days had written: 'I like special well Dorothy Coly: I pray you be good to her.' It was this faithful house servant who later, amidst their grief, prepared More's body for burial. Dame Alice More, his wife, was remembered, as well as his first wife, Jane Colt, who had died years before, and was

buried in the Old Church. I was glad to remember there
More's loved daughter, Margaret Roper, and what he had
written to her: 'Meg, thou hast long known my heart';
and in his last letter, on the day before his execution,
conscious of surrounding guards and their halberds: 'I
never liked your manner toward me better than when you
kissed me last, for I love when daughterly love and dear
charity hath no leisure to look to worldly courtesy.' The
fine spirit and dignity of 'The Man for All Seasons' (made
real to me in the film of that title), came anew in that place
of proud remembering.

Many others – worshippers in the Old Church at some
time since those centuries – were similarly remembered by
the skilled stitchers of the beautiful kneelers, with each
bearing a design and words carefully researched, suitable
to the worshipper. A queen, noblemen, noblewomen, sea-
faring men, and shy people, alike were there remembered.

One of the most attractive to me, and one of whom I
knew nothing before, was Richard Guildford. My time in
Chelsea Old Church, I felt, made that day memorable,
if only for acquaintance with him. His joy in life pro-
claimed had not waited on a gaily-stitched kneeler there in
this century. He lived between 1614 and 1680, and, in a
moment of rare perception, fashioned his own memorial.
And it was a living, timeless expression of feeling: year
by year on his wedding day, *he had made a gift to his
loved church, to mark his happy marriage.*

I am surprised, as I think of thankful Richard Guildford,
that other churchmen, in countless churches since, have
not copied him. But it is not, I persuade myself, too late.
And I can't think of a better idea waiting for three
centuries, for widespread acceptance.

Marriage is more than moonlight, of course – much
more. I have never married; but I have long had friends in
that 'blessed state', and I am a keen observer. Some of
my friends, alas, have been driven to seek release from

86

that early-sought relationship, that for them, in time, has proved impossible. Many a one – seated before my fire with a cup of coffee, or on a well-secreted walk in the countryside – has shared her troubles. I have kept their confidences, but with grief. I have found myself at times poring over Dr Harry Fosdick's words – I wonder if he is right? Of marriage, he says: 'It is not marriage that fails; it is the people that fail. All that marriage does is to show them up.' Some, of course, may enter into this God-ordained relationship too early, or too easily; some even forgetting that it is something to be worked at from both sides, as is any good relationship – friendship, business, or any other. Two persons, I have observed, can set off together round the world, on travel visas and tickets paid in advance, and come back disillusioned, apart. I could put names to a number – already I have listened to their tales.

I rejoice to say that I have many more friends like Richard Guildford, who, despite the tests of years, all the ups-and-downs of sickness, moods, and monetary insecurity, have found love enough. 'A happy marriage is a long conversation that always seems too short', are the words Maurois used. Most of my friends are not poets, and would sooner, like Richard Guildford, put their thanksgiving into some carefully thought out act, or acts. And I'm sure there is a lot to be said for it – even for a literal copying of good Richard's idea of year by year, on his wedding day, giving a gift to his loved church.

Even those of us who are not married, I am certain, are not left outside this glorious experience of thanksgiving. Life is larger than marriage, or singleness, and one prayer given us for constant use, not just for some high moment, makes no mention of either as a condition: 'Grant unto us, O Lord, the royalty of inward happiness, and the serenity which comes from living close to Thee. Daily renew in us the sense of joy, and let Thy eternal spirit dwell in our souls and bodies, filling every corner of our hearts with light and gladness: so that, bearing about with us the infection of a good courage, we may be diffusers of life, and meet all that comes, of good or ill, even death itself, with gallant and high-hearted happiness: *giving Thee thanks for all things.*'

That is the spirit of Richard Guildford, behind which his thanksgiving became over the years an annual celebration. And I like that – for giving thanks is not an act of a moment, though it may start as that: it's an attitude of spirit all the time. Richard Guildford has reminded me of it every year since the one that saw me kneeling in Chelsea Old Church.

The heart, I am fully persuaded as I journey through this wonderful world, needs its anniversaries of thanksgiving. The word has long been with us; it is only its translation into some annual act of gladness that awaits us. It must not be overlooked that – as for Richard Guildford – the word 'anniversary' is built up from the Latin *annus* (a year) tied closely to *versus*, meaning 'turned'. A marriage day, a birthday, or any other day of the year especially meaningful, can serve. To feel strong clean blood pulsing through one's body is a reminder; or to look upon one face beloved, growing older, calmer with the years; one sight of the return of spring, with emergence of scent and colour in one's garden, is enough; a thrush at dawn, a rainbow span spelling out the hope that lives ever in one's human heart, is enough; God sends me so many reminders – even gifts and graces unnumbered that I take of right: a good meal, lovingly served; a story that sends laughter through the room; a book enjoyed, and shared; a piece of music that comes by way of an instrument played, or a radio concert, drifting into the intimate circle; a loved picture on my wall; a cushion with a colourful cover, the work of a craftswoman's nimble fingers. I have no chance of forgetting to give thanks.

I BELIEVE . . . IN MERCY

As we turn these pages that we are sharing, and come upon this chapter heading, one might at first feel it too obvious to be stated. But we live in a world where Mercy, in many countries, is equated with weakness. Looking back over our shoulders, it is not long since German schoolchildren were supplied with textbooks which carried the statement: 'The teaching of Mercy is foreign to the German race, and is, according to the Nordic sentiment, an ethic for cowards and idiots.' We came to know, in time, as indeed did those children growing up in that philosophy, the hideous cost of it, in terms of death and destruction. Many individuals in Germany, we know, refused to think as instructed – and many gave up their lives doing so. We think of men like martyred Bonhoeffer, and women like gracious Mother Maria, martyr of Ravensbrück concentration camp. These refused the philosophy of the merciless – because they were Christians. But hate, violence and grim brutality activated many, so that not only escaping Jews were involved. Terrible things were done by people indoctrinated against Mercy. But if one goes to Dachau today – the setting of many dastardly deeds in terms of gas-chambers and mounds of human ashes – it is to find a prayer inscribed on a memorial bronze; and it is a prayer far removed from the death-dealing philosophy taught those German children. It is a prayer that, no matter where we live, you and I must go on praying:

> May the power
> of Force be overcome:

and Fate yield
to the law
of Justice and Mercy.

This is a worldwide need, more urgent than in many of the
centuries past – and a personal need. On both levels, it is
a conception *based on the very character of God our
Creator, the Redeemer*. In the Bible, that all too few of us
read too seldom, are these ageless words: '*Who is a God
like unto Thee, that pardoneth iniquity, and passeth by
the transgression of the remnant of His heritage? He
retaineth not His anger for ever, because He delighteth in
mercy*' (Micah 7:18 A.V.). I like especially those last
words: 'He delighteth in mercy.' Mercy is no matter of
compulsion, rather of love, of choice, of delight. And this
is the God with Whom we have to deal in our daily life
– in our turn receiving Mercy, and giving Mercy. The
Psalmist speaks of it in words that come down to us as
part of the ongoing human race, to be accepted by Faith:
'The Mercy of the Most High'. Wonderful words, for a
wonderful reality! Without God's Mercy none of us can
live. Or die (Psalm 21:7 A.V.).

Our Master carried this forward in unmistakable clarity:
'Blessed are the merciful, for they shall obtain Mercy
(Matthew 5:7 A.V.).

I rejoice today that there are many people who, like
myself, can say: 'I believe in Mercy' – despite what the
mass media constantly suggest. Even away back in those
grim war days, resulting from that terrible German
philosophy, there were some. A young English soldier of
nineteen, wounded and taken prisoner, wrote to assure his
parents of this (Mr and Mrs Gaines, of Fifteenth Avenue,
Leeds). Of a German soldier from the other side, he said:
'He carried me for seventy yards to the beach, then looked
down at me, smiled, put a cigarette in my mouth, lit it
and put his lighter in my pocket. Then he took off his

white shirt, tore it into shreds and dressed my wounds.'
That part of the story of Normandy, neither he nor his
parents will ever forget. That is Mercy expressed by one
ordinary man for another – and it was multiplied over and
over in those days.

It was happening at the same time, and over a long
time, by many another, knowing well the words of our
Lord. Robert Cross – a worshipper and Sunday School
teacher, a Methodist – is a shining example. For thirty-
one years, he was coxswain of the Humber lifeboat station,
and only retired in 1943. People talk about being 'at the
mercy of the sea' – but the sea is merciless, it has no
mercy. What Mercy is there shown, is in the heart of a
man like Robert Cross. During his years of service he
gave his skills and energies, his very being (to rescue four
hundred and three lives). A brief excerpt from one of the
records of 1940 shines out from these rescues. 'They had
to get out of the surf, for they were on a lee shore. The
rope from the stern was cut and immediately the lifeboat
swung into the shallows and bumped on the sands, split-
ting her rudder and damaging her stern post. It was a
critical position. Fortunately, the boat still responded to
the helm. Somehow they got out of the broken water and
were able to reach the rope fouling the propeller, and cut
it away. Their troubles were ending; with both engines
running, they ran for Grimsby. They had been out for
three and a half hours and had spent ninety minutes in
the actual rescue. Folk who helped them to tie up in
Grimsby Basin said *the lifeboatmen were suffering more
severely and looked more exhausted than the rescued men.*'
The Institution described the service as 'one of the most
difficult and gallant rescues in the history of the Lifeboat
Service', and added that 'the coxswain's courage, endur-
ance and skill were beyond praise'. Added to the great
quality of Christian concern, that my dictionary defines
as *Mercy* – 'the act of relieving suffering, or the disposition

to relieve it' – those qualities referred to, became something very wonderful to that crew of men in the grip of the merciless sea. It is good to have such service recorded. So many acts of Mercy in our everyday life go unrecorded.

Dr J. W. Stevenson, whilst he occupied the editorial chair of a distinguished church paper, rejoiced to tell of a happening that touched life under a church window showing the *Merciful Christ*. Of a relatively modern day – as these other instances of Mercy given – it took place in a Glasgow church, that with others opens wide its doors for any needy one who might want to enter to pray. 'One day', said the Doctor, 'a young man was discovered by a casual visitor. He was kneeling before the communion table, weeping bitterly, and could only say that he wanted to speak to a clergyman.

'The minister was not in the church, but his wife was, and the beadle brought her along to see if she could help. She soon discovered the lad was a Roman Catholic, and offered to bring a priest with whom she was acquainted. A phone call to the RC presbytery brought no result; the priest was out. However, there were other presbyteries, and she managed to get in touch with a priest at last. He answered the call immediately, and was soon sitting in the church with the lad, under the window that shows the *Merciful Christ*. [And what could have been more fitting?] For quite a long time they knelt together, until the boy's tears had ceased, and peace came to him. And out of the open doors of the Protestant church went the priest and the comforted boy.'

Three modern expressions of this God-given, Christ-like quality – each close to life, as Mercy is constantly! We might see it more often, if our eyes were truly awake – expressing itself where others suffer, as did the young soldier; where men are at risk of their lives, amidst threshing storms; or when reduced to manly tears, in some overwhelming experience that may or may not send one through the open doors of a church.

The Psalmist's words become our own prayer: 'O satisfy us early with Thy mercy; that we may rejoice and be glad all our days!' (Psalm 90:14 A.V.). We sing: 'There's a wideness in God's mercy . . .' But it has to be mediated through some merciful human being. That's where you and I come in! 'The great need of our modern age', as one has truly said, *is how to find a merciful neighbour.* To repeat: that's where you and I come in!

As I look back on my happily-remembered time in Palestine, it does not surprise me that there is no single mention of a bridge in the New Testament. In Palestine water is scarce, except for the slender Jordan where John baptized, and for the short time in the year when the snows afar begin to melt. The Jordan can be crossed by fords, and the miniature glens, or *wadis*, that run down to the Sea of Galilee, carry little more than a trickle much of the time.

It is very different in my country: without bridges on most of our roadways, it would be impossible to travel far. And to a marked, if not so great, degree, it is true in England. The country is rich in bridges, some of them built, and already serving, before my own country was even discovered. Most were built of stone, many handsomely and gracefully designed, and they have continued to serve through the centuries. Many a one have I crossed on foot, carrying my haversack, with time to linger and consider their usefulness. In Dorset, a signed notice, with the authority of the Court, reminds passers-by of the importance of the bridge, with the plain words: 'Any person wilfully injuring any part of this County's bridge will be guilty of felony and upon conviction be liable to be transported for life.' I've never seen such a notice in my own country.

But, I once bridged our longest, mightiest river, the Waikato, myself. That was during a tramp, haversack on back, to its source. I was accompanied by a friend. We motored along a desert road, till we had a first meeting with the river. There, near a gravel pit, my friend parked his old car, and got out a piece of canvas to tie over our borrowed sleeping-bags. Night came, and the rippling waters of the young river, only a few feet wide at that stage, issued in sound sleep. Next morning, after I had cooked breakfast over a stick fire, and made hot coffee from our boiling billy, we set off on our tramp to the breast of the mountain, and the river's source, the width of the river diminishing with every mile. At last we came on a little clear pool, above small pebbles – a miniature river, not a foot wide, and to my surprise, and delight, I was able to bridge it with my tramping-shoe. As my friend stood looking on, and chuckling at this treatment of the mighty Waikato River, he photographed 'my bridge'. Though we needed no photograph to remember that moment.

But there are bridges in the mind and spirit, as well as in actuality, as these few mentioned. And in the kind of world we live in today, I should think them every bit as important – even more important, perhaps – than those on any map anywhere. The good Bishop Steere, translator and cathedral-builder of an earlier day, knew this – though few did at the time – and left his pleasant and peaceful setting in Lincolnshire, to serve in Central Africa. He became very attached to a number of little slave boys, and set about teaching them to read. After six years' work, he had *Swahili Exercises*, a dictionary, a translation of parts of St Matthew's Gospel, a few other passages of the Bible, and sections of *The Book of Common Prayer* in Swahili, to show for his effort. And the Chief Vizir saw him off for a little 'break' with the telling words: '*You may be building a bridge* over which the thoughts of Zanzibar might pass to England, and English learning and wisdom find their way to Zanzibar.' And so it proved! Men and women, missionary translators, educators, authors and speakers have been doing as much ever since. That is not forgetting the 'bridge building' of doctors, nurses and technicians. To us ordinary people, the challenge comes today clearer than ever.

When Dr Leslie Weatherhead was made President of the British Methodist Church, he broadcast his first official sermon from Wesley's Chapel, London, on 'Bridge building'. He saw it as the most important task of his ministry during that special year of leadership. And, of course, it didn't end there. He was not thinking only of the historic gap between Anglicans and Methodists, or between warring nations. Bridge building is a continuing task to which we must all give our energies. 'I am asking you', he began, 'to do all you can to bridge the gulf that separates us from those lovable, attractive, often very fine people who are estranged from the churches. We need what they can give us, and they need what we can give them.' Then he spoke of some of the things that separated them – and which needed to be bridged over. Some people, he had discovered, were separated from those in the Church by intellectual doubts; some by fear of disapproval; others by a daily gulf of loneliness – many found it hard, and in some cases impossible, to communicate. Dr Weatherhead finished: '*How badly we need bridges!* Bridges mean fellowship, and it is lack of fellowship that is spoiling our world. Sit down tonight and write a letter, and make it up with anyone in the world with whom you have quarrelled.'

And there are scores of ways of doing this. We can write; we can telephone; we can pay a visit by modern transport; we can draw close through art, music, through some form of social service; through hospital or institutional visitation; through sharing a hobby, or lending an enjoyable book. Our Lord managed His bridge building without any of the modern facilities that are ours. We need, above all, His spirit. He stopped one midday at a well in Sychar (that I have since visited) and bridged over the long-established gap that existed between Himself (a man, a Jew, an acknowledged enemy of all Samaritans) and a Samaritan woman, alone there with her water-pot in the hot midday. He asked of her a drink (John 4:1–30 A.V.).

And today, there is nothing like a simple request for service of some sort – a needed direction as one travels oneself; temporary shelter in a storm; the loan of a daily newspaper somehow missed. Jesus was good at getting close to people, establishing a bridge over an awkward gap. A few words with a little tax-gatherer up a tree, an expressed desire for a meal in his house – and for Zacchaeus everything was changed!

We don't need to be specially trained in the service of His Church today to do this – though the ancient word for priest is *pontifex*, which literally means 'bridge builder'. Dr Paul Tournier, the noted Christian doctor of our day, who has experienced miracles of relationship that lead to healing, and has written of them, declares that life, in order to be life, must know *dialogue*, *'a bridge'*. Isolation spells disaster. And the supreme 'bridge', he says, is dialogue with God – which is communion; the Gospel of Christ in all its wonder – incarnated, coming close, serving, sharing, dying, rising again, offering by Faith all that He is, and all that He has. A 'bridge' – a gift of God in this life of ours – helps to lead us over the chasm of Time into Eternity, which is the fullest Life and Joy we can ever know!

I BELIEVE . . . IN FELLOWSHIP

Words so easily spring to our lips at times — some of them the loveliest words in our language. But we use them often too lightly. One is the word 'Fellowship'. We have our 'Women's Fellowship', our 'Youth Fellowship', our 'Writers' Fellowship'. But Fellowship is something much more than mere proximity. It isn't enough just to get people of one interest together in one place. I learned that whilst in Switzerland. I was in the lovely city of Zürich, and I went for a three-day bus trip with others into the mountains.

We set off early in the morning, as arranged. The air was all that mountain air can be, as we rode with the top of the bus open. But I was the only passenger without any Swiss-German. When we stopped mid-morning for coffee, I had to consult the driver about the length of time we meant to stay — and at what time we were to go on. Holding up my watch for his scrutiny, and pointing at it with my forefinger, I uttered one word, 'When?' (meaning when would we reassemble for the bus?). Using his finger in the same way, to point to a figure on my watch, he said but one English word: 'Him!' So I knew — following the same procedure each time we stopped — that when 'When?' was 'Him', it was when!

I enjoyed my three carefree days with those happy people, who talked and sang as we wove our way through the passes, and up the sides of mountains affording distant blue views, each to sleep each night in a different chalet, in a different bed. Nobody but the bus driver spoke a word to me — nobody could, they had no English. So nobody asked me if I liked the mountains, or commented on the weather, or asked me what I thought about the govern

ment, or asked me if I was a churchwoman, or how many
children I had, or whether I'd like the window closed.
I'd just finished an exacting lecture tour in Britain, and it
was bliss to be with this lively company. We were together,
listening to the same things, looking at the same things,
going the same way – but it wasn't exactly what one could
call 'Fellowship' – *it was only proximity!*

And that is what many of our Fellowship gatherings,
I fear, amount to. We get people together – but again and
again, something is lacking. We don't quite manage to
make actual what that word in the Psalms means: 'How
rare it is, how lovely the fellowship of those who meet
together' (Psalm 133:1 Moffatt), much less the New
Testament *koinonia*. Our need, as human beings, lies in
– to use Harold Louke's clear way of putting it – 'the fact
that we learn to love by loving and being loved; the fact
that the private conscience is never sensitive enough alone;
that the personal will is never strong enough alone; that
the widely concerned individual can only specialize on one
or two of his concerns . . . If the Church did not exist it
would be necessary to invent it.' He is thinking of 'the
fellowship of believers', of loving, concerned, outreaching
people, as from the beginning it was intended to be, and
wherever one finds it at its best, it is!

There is no such person as a 'solitary Christian' – we
need fellowship; it is essential to our way of life. That
has been recognized from the beginning. Paul wrote to his
friends: 'I want to be among you to be myself encouraged
by your faith, as well as you by mine' (Romans 1:12, as
translated in The New English Bible). As this need is basic
to all Christians – loving people, awkward people, shy
people, self-assured people, young and old – *koinonia* is not
just the feeling of having a jolly time together, it is a
deep-down sense of one-ness in a life experience, a realization of being united in Christ, and in faith together. And
this is a wonderful kind of fellowship, unmatched at any

other level. It is something more than making up differences of opinion, of finding a mateyness between master and worker, rich and poor, hippy and square, black and white. It may do all of this – but it is something much more. To borrow Paul's words on yet another occasion: 'If there is any fellowship in the Spirit . . .', he added, writing to his friends in Philippi, 'complete my joy by being of the same mind, having the same love' (Philippians 2 : 1–2 R.S.V.). Fellowship is so much more than tacking a label on people, who, for any cause, are brought together, especially within the Church. It is impossible, of course, for shallow persons, self-opinionated, selfish – since so little depends on proximity. My dictionary defines Fellowship as 'participation, intercourse, friendliness' – but even that, in actuality, leaves much unsaid, to anyone experiencing Christian Fellowship, where it is warm and living.

One day Bishop Lesslie Newbigin told us of a wonderful experience he had in his diocese in India. He was new to his life as a bishop when the United Church of South India came into being, and he found himself appointed. He made an introductory tour to get to know something of the challenge he faced. At every village the Christian people came out to meet him, and this was good. In one village the Christians were led by an extraordinary character, clad in an old Royal Air Force uniform, and carrying, surprisingly, a stainless steel baton. With this, he controlled those who came with him; at a sign from him, they knelt; at another, they rose. Bishop Newbigin was curious to know what lay behind this irregular behaviour in a Christian gathering. Staying with him later, it all came out – and a wonderful story it was, an instance of rich Fellowship that overleapt many differences. His name was Sundarum. At the beginning of the Second World War, it transpired, he was preaching the Gospel in Burma, and in the advance of the Japanese armies, he was captured, and taken to a guard post. Everything he carried was taken from him, he was cruelly bound, and thrown into a corner. Presently a Japanese officer came in. He went to the table where Sundarum's scanty possessions lay. Among them was a worn Tamil Bible. The officer knew no word of Tamil, but he recognized the book as a Bible; and holding up his hand, and tracing on his palm the sign of the Cross, he looked questioningly towards Sundarum. Sundarum knew no word of Japanese, but he knew that the officer was asking him if he was a Christian, and he nodded. At that point, the officer walked across the room, and stood in front of his prisoner, stretched out his arms in the form of the Cross, then cut Sundarum's bonds, and restoring to him his few possessions, bade him go. And he did more. Before they parted – two Christian men, with a thousand differences, but one essential shared – he handed to Sundarum, as a token of that reality, his officer's staff, and this was now the stainless steel baton with which Sundarum directed his loved congregation. Between these two men was, in the circumstances of war, a gulf that one would have thought beyond bridging – *but in the Fellowship of Christ, it was not so.* No wonder Sundarum treasured his baton, and his loved congregation, too. And young Bishop Lesslie Newbigin told of it as one of the great moments of his Christian sharing. Paul would have loved it, just as much, and would have written it into one of his New Testament letters, as Doctor Luke would have written it into the New Testament book of Acts. In my turn, I write it into this book – and it leaves me feeling that there are no situations where Fellowship of the kind I have been reminded of, cannot be meaningful.

'*I believe . . . in Fellowship!*' A friend of mine in Canada, Asa Johnson, wrote of it truly:

There is a closeness in the Fellowship
of Christian folk
that does not come from excellence

I Believe Here and Now

in us, our ways,
the record of our lives,
or what we plan to do;
it comes from Christ,
living within our lives,
drawing us closer to Himself
and nearer to each other.

Beauty isn't a pleasant extra – it's a living essential. The world round, the seasons round, in experience after experience, I find myself taking the words of the Psalmist upon my lips: *'Let the beauty of the Lord our God be upon us'* (Psalm 90:17 A.V.). Charles Kingsley, whatever he prayed in private, was once heard to exclaim amid bud and blossom: 'How beautiful God is! How beautiful God is!' For a Creator cannot in Himself be less beautiful than what He creates! Was it, I wonder, the freshness of the dawn, or the contour of the hills, that moved the Psalmist, as so often they move me?; or the sweep of a hastening stream to a clear pool's depths? Or was it in some minute form of beauty – moss or lichen?; or the splendid joy of a craftsman?; or the lithe muscles of a fit youth? The sky at sundown?; or the respected honour of a silvered head? Beauty of God's giving comes so variously, in shapes, textures, proportions, colours, purposes.

Men and women, from the beginning of time, have tried to match it by the human shortcut of cosmetics. The Egyptians favoured kohl-darkened eyes, and henna-bright hair. St Jerome, in his day, objected to the practice of people around him who made use of rouge. There was no hiding the fact that such 'beauty' was superficial in every way. And the immense, world-wide business that has grown out of it today must admit as much.

The beauty most to be rejoiced in is from within, and is God's gift, a gift of the spirit. It shows itself *in love, in courage, in forgiveness, in caring, and in goodness that is gracious*. And one by one, I find myself thinking of these qualities as I've come across them.

First, I rejoice in 'the beauty of the Lord our God', as

shown in Love. I could instance it as between two young people, fresh, and beautifully awakened to each other; or the beauty of mother love or father love. But for an expression of love, in the least attractive setting, boundlessly and beautifully sustained, let me introduce Samuel Barnett, vicar of St Jude's, in the East End of London, later Warden of Toynbee Hall. Out of a deep love for God and people, he poured out, day after day, after day, after day, a particular kind of living. Many, evincing interest, came down from the affluent West End to see what he and his wife were doing – to offer advice, and occasionally even a blue-print plan for the redemption of their dreary slum. But such casuals did not stay. They did not give themselves. The only good ever offered the Warden and his people, as Mrs Barnett underlined, was done 'by those who were willing to take time and trouble with individuals'. *This required Love, that beautiful gift of God, expressed in human experience, without measure.*

Then I think of the rare beauty of courage – and my mind flies to one and another, in an ordinary enough experience of invalidism. One, a double-amputee as a result of war, who week by week came up our five front doorsteps, with a brown paper bag of eggs for our larder. And never a complaint or word of self-pity escaped him. But I will instance a more public kind of courage displayed by a woman, but a few years in my own country, New Zealand. For courage is in no sense a male gift, of course. Here, the National Council of Churches sponsors, from time to time, outsiders in sad trouble. The Report says: '*Most show wonderful Courage* . . . One of them is Adela Sipoecz from Poland. Along with many other Poles, she was deported as slave labour to Germany. There she married a fellow Polish slave labourer. Unfortunately, he was killed in an air raid.

'With the defeat of Germany, Adela returned to Poland, only to be arrested by the Russians. She managed to escape, and after many adventures reached West Germany, where she got jobs as a seamstress, factory worker and engine-driver.

'In 1953 she married a Hungarian, but after only a few years of marriage he contracted TB and died. Such a loss, in addition to all her previous trials, would have driven most people to despair. But Adela refused to give up, and eventually applied to come as a refugee to New Zealand.

'Sponsored by the Society of Friends in Dunedin, she arrived in September 1964. Professor Smithells of Dunedin says: "She is a remarkable woman. She arrived without knowledge of English, but at once set about learning the language. She then studied and passed all her examinations in psychiatric nursing, and is now Night Sister in Ashburn Hall in Dunedin." '

And the beauty of *Forgiveness* is as truly of the very nature of God – a gift to human spirits here and now. Only one petition of 'The Lord's Prayer' actually has a condition attached, and it is this offering and receiving of Forgiveness. 'Forgive us . . . as we forgive' is part of the Prayer given us by our Lord. 'If you forgive others the wrongs they have done to you, your Father in heaven will also forgive you. But if you do not forgive others, then your Father will not forgive the wrongs you have done' (Matthew 6:14–15 Good News Bible). God has created this world, and our living within it, on a family basis.

> 'Tis sweet to stammer one letter
> Of the Eternal's language, on earth,
> It is called *Forgiveness*.

In the words of one amongst us:

> Forgiveness is not easy,
> not if you're hit hard,
> hurt by cruel spite;

or worse, someone near and dear
harmed irreparably by malice,
careless apathy,
or just plain stupidity.

But there's another harder thing to do,
and that's to seek forgiveness
even as a leaden load of guilt
hangs on your sinking heart:
to make that awkward move of reconciliation,
blushing with blame,
dreading rebuff,
fearing the worst.

Lord, You forgave even from the Cross.
Give me the bigness of heart
to follow Your example;
and more,
let me so love my neighbour
as to forget my pride.

(Anon.)

There is also the beauty of *Caring* that I have mentioned.
This is no easy thing either, in many expressions of it. It
is easy to care for those who care for us – but there are
the others. I realized this anew as I listened to Dr Donald
Soper of London speak, on this side of the world, of a
piece of social work in what he called 'the Mission where
I work'. 'In an old and transformed nineteenth-century
casualty ward we *seek to care* for more than a hundred
destitute people . . . Technically, they are entitled to the
sort of help that the Welfare State offers in its various
institutions. Practically, because of mental peculiarities or
personal habits, these most unfortunate people, both men
and women, are unacceptable in any of the State-provided
hostels. Putting it bleakly, if they were housed in these

institutions the other inmates would raise bitter and continuous complaint . . . The hostel represents the continuing need *for someone to care* . . . When talking about this piece of work, I come across those who say how wonderful it must be to have a hand in such romantic service, how lovely it must be to tend these sad old people, and to see their wrinkled faces break into smiles of gratitude. I wish it were like this,' Dr Soper was obliged to finish, 'but it's not. Most of the people cared for in the Hungerford Hostel are not lovely or grateful, but warped and grudging and unpleasant.' But still, men and women with God's gift of caring deep in their spirits, go on – and there is an undoubted beauty in that. It is a God-like gift. Isaiah speaks of 'the Eternal so rich in care for us' (Isaiah 63:7 Moffatt). But for a full understanding of that care, and the unending costliness of it, we have to turn to the New Testament. For a Cross stands there!

And I want to mention, too, *the Goodness that is Gracious*. In Mayfield I came across monuments to the Baker family – and one that I shall never forget. It said of John Baker: 'He was good, and did good.' The only question that rose instinctively in my mind was, 'Was his goodness gracious?' Or harsh, and unfeeling – as much alleged 'goodness' through the years has been? When Florence Allshorn, founder of St Julian's, was in West Africa on service, she had dealings with a company of Christians, and had to write of them: 'You're all so good. Everywhere I go, everyone is up so early, so busy, so good . . . Yet . . .' For beyond that point something was lacking – they lacked what men and women saw in Christ; what Paul wrote to his friends: 'You know *how gracious* our Lord Jesus Christ was' (2 Corinthians 8:9 Moffatt). In Greek there are two words for good: there is *agathos*, scholars remind us, which describes a thing morally good. And there is *kalos*, which describes a thing not only good *but beautiful*. A relationship, an action, might be *agathos*, and yet be hard, stern, unattractive. But a thing which is *kalos* is winsome.

A simple question that someone – aware of all this of which I have enjoyed writing – has fashioned, a question that might well be on the lips of each of us, concerning Christian beauty:

> Lord, is my life so full of Thee
>   That others, walking with me, see
> Some beauty of the Life divine
>   Revealed through mine?

I BELIEVE . . . IN HOSPITALITY

I have journeyed many miles in many countries, and stayed in many homes. Some of them have been in great cities, with the thunder of traffic, some in the quietness of the countryside, with the fragrance of gardens through open windows at night-fall, and birdsong to waken me in the morning. Some of the houses have been old – admittedly inconvenient – brick and stone, warmed and tested by centuries of sun and storm; others have been new, with exactly the right coloured benchtops, floor coverings and restful lampshades. 'Pleasantest of all ties, is the tie of host and guest.'

I have often wondered about the homes into which Paul and his colleagues entered in the early days of the Church. For lodging places were few then, and often of very doubtful character. It was so much better to stay with fellow believers, if that could be arranged. And since communication between them was fragmentary, and the very fact of being counted Christians very dangerous, in those early times, fellowship on both sides was precious. Paul required this of any bishop, along with other graces, and made it clear to young Timothy, setting out in his ministry: 'A bishop then must be blameless, the husband of one wife, vigilant, sober, of good behaviour, *given to hospitality* . . .' (1 Timothy 3:2 A.V.). This hospitality was required not only of leaders in the Church, but of all who professed Christian discipleship: 'rejoicing in hope, patient in tribulation; continuing instant in prayer; distributing to the necessity of saints; *given to hospitality*' (Romans 12:12–13 A.V.). Many of these lived in modest homes, but even there hospitality was one of earth's best gifts. We are given no description as to whether the homes were in the hot, crowded cities visited by Paul and his colleagues, or in pleasant suburbs, with cool vines over the portico and hangings handwoven. No menu has been preserved, but we assume there was always food served to support good talk. Some of the homes may have been poor, with sun-blistered walls, and set in little, mean streets.

What kind of houses, I wonder, did they live in, those friends named by Paul at the end of his letters – Stephanus of Corinth; Fortunatus of that same great heathen city? We don't know where Achaicus lived. We wish we did; it would be easier to visualize the setting, though we are sure of the warmth of his welcome. Paul's visit happened so seldom. Paul has told us only one lovely fact of those who received him: '*They refreshed my spirit*' (1 Corinthians 16:18 R.S.V.).

Where such refreshment was lacking – for in those long journeys the travellers must sometimes have been dis-appointed – it could only have been, as now, where nothing but food and shelter was available. These alone could not have earned that lovely tribute of thanks: '*They refreshed my spirit!*'

Does this bring us to the very heart of that much-misunderstood story of Mary and Martha? Our Lord, wearied with travel, was not disdainful of food and com-fort; but what He needed even more was refreshment of spirit. A heart at leisure from itself, He needed, ease; a mind interested in the things that mattered to Him, fellow-ship; a spirit pervading the place with a gentle happiness as natural as the air waiting to be breathed, love. This Mary, to her lasting praise, understood. And Stephanus and Fortunatus and Achaicus understood. They offered the greatest thing possible to their guest.

No wonder our Lord's hospitable word, which has come down to us, in our need, centres right here: 'Come unto Me, and *I will refresh you*' (Matthew 11:28 Moffatt). He now, as then, has no home of His own – so His words have a deeper level of meaning.

There have always been lonely people moving from place to place, in the execution of their routine responsibilities, or in pursuit of new opportunities and relationships. And life for some of these is, to this day, discoloured and made more difficult by hospitality refused. In the New Testament is a striking example of this in the experience of our Lord and His disciples. As Dr William Barclay has reminded us in his book, *The Mind of Jesus* (S.C.M. Press): 'On the road to Jerusalem, Jesus and His men came to a Samaritan village. They requested hospitality, and not surprisingly – ' because we think of the old feud between Jews and Samaritans – 'they were rebuffed. Thereupon James and John wished to call down fire from heaven, to obliterate the inhospitable village, but Jesus forbade it' (Luke 9:51–56 A.V.).

But hospitality, in its fullest Christian sense, means more than bed and lodging, even with good food and talk. It reaches out to receiving others in their need, in our prayers. In *The Genesee Diary*, on a stay in a Trappist Monastery, by a young Dutch priest, Henri Nouwen (Doubleday), I found this reality. And it has special significance in this day when lonely hearts are so many, and so widely spread. Reporting a seven-month retreat experience, he says: 'I had a very vivid realization that I must create some free space in my innermost self so that I may indeed invite others to enter and be healed. To pray for others means *to offer others a hospitable place where I can really listen to their needs and pains.*'

Mary of Bethany understood this – though many of us are not yet fully grasping it. But it is an essential of the kind of hospitality that refreshens worn spirits. Outside the New Testament, I was delighted to come across the witness of Cyprian. Said he (dating his letter from Carthage, in the year AD 250), 'It is a bad world, Donatus, an incredibly bad world. But I have discovered in the midst of it a quiet and holy people who have learned a great secret. They have found a joy which is a thousand times better than any of the pleasures of our sinful life. They are despised and persecuted, but they care not. They are masters of their own souls. They have overcome the world. These people, Donatus, are Christians – *and I am one of them!*' Isn't that a warm, live, refreshing claim? To come travel-worn to the house of Cyprian could only spell refreshment – the very soul of hospitality.

To miss this is to miss an essential in life. God made us to share not only things, but our very selves – the warm realities of mind and spirit, and all that nourishes them. So conversation, and the exchange of books, and music, and experiences, and crafts, and acquired qualifications, can mean much. One can understand what this meant to Paul, the missionary, tent-maker and traveller. Perhaps he was thinking of some of those refreshing times in homes where he had entered a stranger, and left a deeply-loved friend, when he wrote to young Timothy, in another of his letters: '*God . . . giveth us richly all things to enjoy.*' He Who made us for individual response, I believe, is every bit as much honoured by our 'togetherness' – our 'hospitality' (1 Timothy 6:17 A.V.).

'*I believe in Hospitality!*'

To many, nothing is so unwelcome as a new thought. There are some wonderful things that God cannot do in this world, until men love; and there are some exciting things He cannot do, until we think. Truth comes often in unexpected shapes and forms – even in the distasteful task of thinking things over again. It takes courage to offer hospitality to a fresh idea.

It takes courage to say: 'I believe in Hospitality!'

Laughter enlarges my landscape —
   quickens my hearing, my sight,
refreshes my spirit's colours,
   bringing me each day new delight.

In childhood, I prayed to be rich,
   but that prayer has now long ended —
since work and leisure, joy and love
   and laughter my heart befriended.

                        (R.F.S.)

Refreshing laughter is as old as time — one of God's good gifts. If it didn't come from Him, where indeed did it come from? He knew from the beginning that life would sometimes hold days difficult for us without it. I say 'refreshing laughter', because there have developed many kinds. 'As the crackling of thorns under a pot,' says an early Bible passage, *'so is the laughter of a fool'* (Ecclesiastes 7:6 A.V.).

Then there is the laughter of incredulity. When God made a promise to an elderly couple, it was said: 'Abraham fell upon his face, and laughed . . . "Shall a child be born unto him that is an hundred years old? And shall Sarah, that is ninety years old, bear?" ' (Genesis 17:17 A.V.).

Further on in the same great record of human behaviour, is a note on a valiant soul, who setting out to re-build his beloved but demolished city, met with *'the laughter of scorn'* (Nehemiah chapter 6 A.V.). Nehemiah's record is, word for word, one of the most exciting and glorious in history — I never tire of it. Happily Nehemiah — with the grace of God — found strength to overcome the damning laughter that his so-called 'friends' brought against him!

And from every age since, and among us today, we might instance kinds of laughter. But without it, at its best, we lack an essential in our living. 'There is in God', one has said, 'a well of laughter very deep.' We may never have thought of God like this; yet we know, as the outcome of years' experience here, that one can be serious without being solemn. We know that laughter of the best kind clears the spirit of petty pride and simpering impatience, as thunder clears the air. Introduced into a day's hard dealings, it has the power to heal, in the place of hurt – a God-like quality. Such laughter, said Dr C. S. Lewis, is rightly to be received as 'from the God Who made good laughter'.

This being so, it comes to us as something of a surprise that *there is a right time and a wrong time for laughter*. You may have been as fortunate as I, in being reminded of this by Tom Skillen, on the BBC. Life had been harsh enough for him, and varied enough. He talked about his early youth; his helping to run a stall in Old Caledonian Market, London; his soldiering; and what specially took my attention, helping his father in his shop. 'One afternoon', said he, 'a tubby little lady brought in her husband's boots for soling and heeling. Early next morning, she panted back into the shop. "Started 'em?" she gasped. Dad answered, "No". "Thank goodness – only do the right one; he's been run over, and might lose his left leg."

'She was soon gone – and we were silent. I didn't know whether to laugh or not . . . Many years later', he added 'I opened the shop to find a darkly dressed lady sitting on the doorstep. I knew her well. She was very old and lived alone. She came in, slumped into a chair, and pointed wearily to her foot encased in a zipped bootee.

' "Get it off," she pleaded. The zip was so jammed I had to cut it to oblige. "Bless you, Tommy boy," she said. "

couldn't have gone to bed another night in it." She passed me a cough-drop, and hobbled out. I stood grinning as I imagined the old lady going to bed with a boot on. Then suddenly, the stark tragedy of the affair hit me . . . the misery of being friendless and helpless. *I had been doing a lot of laughing in the wrong places.*

That can happen anywhere. It's one thing to laugh *with* people – another to laugh *at* them. That can be cruel and dispiriting – and laughing was never meant to be that. Rather was it meant to be refreshing, supporting, renewing. This kind of laughter is nearer than anything to what old Thomas Hobbes called 'a sudden glory'. That's as good a name for laughter as any coined through the years. Instant in clearing dullness, in disposing of the pompous, the hypocritical, the patronizing, there is no better way of bringing one to a good, living sense of proportion.

Curiously, laughter is about the last thing that many expect in church – but others have become more realistic about this gift of God. Dr Helmut Thielicke, the distinguished European preacher, scholar and author, from Hamburg, was lately in our city, and I went to hear him, having a number of his books on my shelves. As well as preaching regularly to a congregation of four thousand, he is a professor at the university. In his book on the Apostles' Creed I was interested to find him writing of laughter. 'Medieval Christians,' he was pleased to remind us, 'before they were petrified by liturgical gravity, knew what they called the *risus paschalis*, that resounded through the Churches. The Eastern Church', he was glad to add, 'still observes this custom, even though it is a persecuted church. That laughter', he finished, 'praises the Father Who snatched His Son from the grip of Death, and made a laughing-stock of the world and all its fury.'

Of all people the earth round, the seasons round, Christians ought surely to be the best at handling exacting situations – we ought to know when God's good gift of laughter can help. Sullen saints do not know such a secret and are in themselves a contradiction in terms. Laughter as nothing else, lets the overcoming triumph and glory of Easter through – dismissing things fearful, false, pitiful and weak. With the fresh, rich abandon of the triumph of the first Easter morning, that found Mary in the Garden outside the empty tomb, talking to her Risen Lord, a new quality comes into life for us Christians everywhere. I comes with the fresh, rich abandon of spring, sun and wind, a glory of everlasting wonder and triumph!

'For meet it is that the heavens should rejoice', is a line from the Liturgy of the Eastern Church, 'and that the earth should be glad, and that the whole world, both visible and invisible, should keep the Feast. For Christ is risen the everlasting joy.

'Now all things are filled with light, heaven and earth and all the places under the earth. All creation doth celebrate the Resurrection of Christ.

'Rejoice, O creation, and bloom like a lily! For Christ as God has risen from the dead! O death, where is thy sting? O grave, where is thy victory?

'As God Thou didst arise from the grave in glory, and with Thee didst raise the world!'

I BELIEVE . . . IN PEACE-MAKERS

Too easily today, too many of us use the word 'peace' in
a negative sense. Where a lake and its girdling trees before
us are not stirred and smashed by a storm, we say there is
peace; where men and women are not at each others'
throats, or lashing each other in wordy argument, we say
there is peace. But it is not necessarily so. The word 'peace'
rises too easily to our English-speaking tongues; and even,
I suspect, to Jewish tongues. For I remember hearing
Shalom, the Jewish word for 'peace', first from a guard at
the barbed-wire barrier that went by the name of the
Mandelbaum Gate. Palestine, the little land of our Lord
that I had flown half the world for, was torn in two, with
this guarded barbed-wire barrier at its heart. Because no
Arab would look upon a document that a Jew had looked
upon, I carried two wads of air tickets, and two passports
supplied by my country. The word *Shalom*, like so many,
has become conventionalized. In its usage now it has
become a casual greeting, used as freely as we say 'Good
day'. In both Greek and Hebrew, says Dr William Barclay,
"peace" is an intensely positive word. It has two main
meanings – it means "right relationships between man and
man", true fellowship, not just polite tolerance. (In
Matthew 5:9, the translation should be: "O the bliss of
those who make friends with each other.") Again, it means
'everything which makes for one's highest good" . . . The
positive side of the word "peace" must at all times be
stressed.'

This is implied, of necessity, in the Old Testament
prophecy (Micah 4:3 A.V.) when speaking of the nations:
They shall beat their swords into ploughshares, and their
spears into pruning hooks.' There is to be *positive* action.

I Believe Here and Now

Those were the words that faced me – tellingly engraved on a wall across the United Nations Plaza from the UN Headquarters in New York City. At the other corner in the same block stands the Church Centre of the UN, where that ancient prophecy is uplifted, and pondered on, in its proper Biblical setting, leading on to its New Testament meaning for this modern age. Not only in this place, but everywhere, no word of Scripture is read with greater longing than these from Micah. Human hearts cry the world round: 'When will the day come when precious metals will be used for instruments of agriculture, and not for deadly weapons?' Thousands pass by way of the UN Plaza every day, and read those words, and many, as I did, enter the Meditation Room within the great building. It is one thing to chisel the words of a dream in a public place, another to sink it deeply into one's heart and mind, in daily relationships and in national aims. In an attempt to explain its great altar-like block of iron ore at the centre, of the room, Dag Hammarskjöld, General Secretary of UN, said on its opening day: 'In this house we are trying to turn swords into ploughshares. And we thought that we could bless the very material out of which arms are made, iron ore – which represents the very paradox of human life – material offered by God to us, either for construction or for destruction.' It is at this point that the issue waits – dream or nightmare. Some today think that with the weapons science now places in men's hands lies the last chance of humanity. So many attempts at the council table have been foiled by secret ambition, and deeply-laid distrust. But we'll never have a world at peace till swords are turned into ploughshares, missile stations into medical clinics, excessive defence expenditure into hunger and illiteracy relief.

Most of us have now lived through two or more wars in Europe and Asia. We have known the misery attendant on the machines of death; we have not been able anywhere

to escape wireless news plugging away in workshops and
anxious homes, ejecting into every silence its barrage of
propaganda, blotting out the sweet outlines of peace. Said
Dag Hammarskjöld, finishing his speech that day at the
dedication of the Meditation Room (that, surprising many
of us, at first held no Cross): 'Ours is a work of reconciliation and realistic construction.' A plaque there carries
words that Hammarskjöld himself had written:

THIS IS A ROOM DEVOTED
TO PEACE
AND THOSE WHO ARE
GIVING THEIR LIVES
FOR PEACE

IT IS A ROOM OF
QUIET WHERE ONLY
THOUGHT SHOULD SPEAK

The New Testament era, that we have recorded in unforgettable words, opened with the glorious proclamation:
'*Glory to God in the Highest, and on earth peace, good
will toward men*' (Luke 2:14 A.V.). Though these words
are not familiar to those of many nations, of non-Christian
faiths, who use that Meditation Room, we recall them at
Christmas at least, though by too many of us they are but
glibly spoken. We want peace – but on our own terms, it
seems. We do not start with the basic condition, *offering
first Glory to God*. Only after that, as a natural result, can
we rightly expect 'peace on earth'. The worst and most
deadly attitude is to set man in the place that rightly
belongs to God – our plans above His.

On a plaque, as one emerges into the air of common
day coming from that Meditation Room, is a reminder of
the *cost* of being peace-makers. I had, till I stood there,
read those words with the emphasis on the first word

'peace'; but now I read them with the emphasis on the second word 'makers'. For His call is not to 'peace-hopers' or 'peace-eulogizers' – but to *makers* of peace. Dag Hammarskjöld's own name was all too soon added to that plaque, together with the name of Count Bernadotte, the Swedish mediator who gave his life in an effort for peace in the Middle East. With the passage of years since a growing number, a roll of cost, has been added.

Jesus, our Lord, Who first gave the world these words about peace-makers, challenged His followers not only to refrain from hating their enemies in any way – but to *love* them. And He knew it would not be easy; for it is a positive, active relationship, one that He observed all His days on this earth. It begins for us, of course, in the home, and goes out to one's community, the work place, the country, the world. For these all, each in the most real way, we seek God's peace. 'Peace', some bright one has said, 'is not a bottle of milk left on the doorstep while we are asleep.' It is not just a matter of 'nothing bad happening', nor even of 'nothing much happening' – it is a positive quality of life and relationships, '*something good happening!*'

'Blessed are the peace-makers,' are our Lord's words, 'for they shall be called the children of God!'

In our world today one has to admit that by no means everyone holds to this belief. Some accept it as an everyday maxim; others think of people only as they can serve some political or religious end. I must confess I saw little point in a statement by Dame Edith Evans when first I came upon it, but now I see that it is bound up with essential respect. 'People', she holds, *are people wherever you meet them.*

This, I have come to see, is a basic Christian belief. That it is *people* we have dealings with, young or old, English-speaking or not, of white skins, yellow, or red, or darker still, it makes no difference. And we get this lead from our Lord Himself. He longed to gather people into His Kingdom, as leaders or followers – but He never ceased to respect their right of choice. Never once was He tempted to coerce them into discipleship. He knew, as we know, that there are various ways of getting followers. One can impose one's will by sheer physical force; by the power of one's superior personality; by intellectual or by spiritual superiority. Jesus might have fallen back on any one of these means of establishing His desired Kingdom – but He did not. And time was short, too. He chose, rather, the way of respect, though it was a way requiring time and patience, and could never be hurried.

Again and again the New Testament makes His approach plain. Emotionally stirred, a man impulsively offers himself in discipleship; and Jesus urges him *to go home and count the cost.* He wouldn't take advantage of him. He has been granted, as a man, the sacred right of choice, and he should be allowed to exercise it in a cool moment of consideration. To rush him, by any means, into

a decision that on the morrow he would regret, was never
our Lord's way. No one with whom He had dealings, however eager He was for disciples and the progress of His
Kingdom, could ever feel that he was bludgeoned into
service. No one! One thinks of 'the Rich Young Ruler',
who was, on first appearance, exactly the type of candidate
He sought. It is recorded of him that 'he came running'.
Such an eager character! He was young; he was rich; he
was a ruler, with some experience of leadership that would
have been handy in building up a larger and ever larger
following; and that would have been a help. 'But Jesus – '
as Dr William Barclay feels he must point out – 'did two
things that every evangelist and every preacher and every
teacher ought to remember and copy. First, Jesus said in
effect, "Stop and think! You are all wrought up and palpi-
tating with emotion! I don't want you swept to Me by
a moment of emotion. Think calmly what you are doing."
. . . Secondly, Jesus said in effect, "You cannot become a
Christian by a sentimental passion for Me. You must look
at God." The danger is that the pupil, the scholar, the
young person can form a personal attachment to the
teacher or the preacher and think that is an attachment to
God. There is in all true teaching a certain self-obliteration.
True, we cannot keep personality and warm personal
loyalty out of it altogether, and we would not if we could.
But the matter must not stop there. The teacher and the
preacher are in the last analysis only finger-posts to God.'

Nor are eagerness, youth, experience of leadership, and
wealth altogether reason enough for bypassing respect for
a coveted disciple. And, surprisingly, for those who looked
on and did not at that time understand Jesus's deep-down
attitude of respect, this promising young would-be followed
'turned away sorrowfully' (Mark 10 : 17–22 A.V.). But i
couldn't have been otherwise, as Jesus saw things.

One is reminded in the gospels of His attitude to others
I have only space in which to refer to two women an

two men as typical. In His relation to them He was so far
removed from the average religious leader, in every way.
He did not set up in some distant place of seclusion, to be
sought and consulted by those needing His advice. *He
came where the needy were – and met them as they were,
with respect always.* No more surprising example could
anyone have imagined than His meeting with the woman
of Sychar. It was 'about the sixth hour' – with the burning
sun high overhead, when ordinarily nobody came to
Jacob's well to draw water. But here was a woman who,
for her own reasons, came when she had a chance of being
the only one there with a water-pot. At other times people
refused to talk to her, and when she was out of sight,
talked about her. But Jesus, resting on the well-side,
opened up conversation with her. She was a Samaritan, a
long-time enemy of Jesus's people, but more than that a
woman, with whom a religious leader would not ordinarily
speak alone; and she had a very shady moral background.
Jesus knew all these things – but she was a lonely soul.
To her Jesus gave some of His most wonderful teaching on
worship, anywhere recorded (John 4:3–30 A.V.). Despite
all, He respected her as a person with God-given rights.

One can say as much of the woman taken in adultery.
Hers was a sorry story (John 8:3–11 A.V.), and she was
surrounded by salacious accusers, who seemed to have the
Law on their side. She had offended, and they urged her
into the presence of Jesus, hoping to bring charges against
Him, as the result of bringing charges against the woman
and His handling of the situation. But it didn't work. There
was an unknown quality present. Whilst not condoning her
sin, Jesus still saw her as a needy human being, who had
a claim on His respect. He succeeded in making her
accusers uncomfortable, as He lifted His eyes from the
miserable woman and lowered them to write with His
finger in the dust. It was a turn of events that no one
could have imagined. And without that strange quality of

human respect, never would have happened. His final words, when her accusers had departed, with 'their tails between their legs', and He was left alone with her, were: 'I do not condemn you: go and sin no more.' (Both of these people come briefly into the light, and as quickly depart; we see them no more and know nothing more of them. What happened to them, as the days went by, what wonders were worked in them as the result of this loving respect? I wish we could have a postscript to the gospels.)

Another was Matthew, whom a modern scholar was led to introduce as 'the man whom all men despised'. But there was One Man who didn't despise him, Who respected him as a human being. Victor Hugo's word for another character ostracized by his fellows comes tellingly to mind: 'Ignominy is athirst for respect.' I wonder? Anyway, Matthew was a fellow outside the realm of community affection. The outstanding fact was simply that he was a tax-gatherer. That was enough in itself to set people against him. There was no class of men more hated in the ancient world. One can't help saying that they brought it upon themselves. Cicero, in talking of trades and occupations below a gentleman, suggests at once those of a tax-gatherer and usurer. 'Murderers, robbers and tax-gatherers' were commonly classed together. 'A tax-gatherer', one scholar reminds me, 'was debarred from being either a witness or a judge. He was even debarred from worship, which was why the tax-gatherer in the parable stood *afar off* (Luke 18:13 A.V.). Even repentance itself was regarded as being specially difficult for a tax-gatherer. But it was not only on religious grounds that they were hated; they were notoriously rapacious and unjust. When the repentant tax-gatherers asked John the Baptist what they must do, his answer was: "Exact no more than that which is appointed you" (Luke 3:13 A.V.). The Roman method of tax collecting lent itself to abuse.

Under the Republic, the collecting of taxes had been farmed out.'

But Jesus paused to have talk and personal dealings with a fellow far removed from popularity and the straight-dealing that might have earned him better treatment (Matthew 9:9 A.V.). And even further His deep respect went, so that Matthew, the miserable fellow now hating his trade, rose to be a disciple of Jesus. And what a gain that was – to the little band, and to us all, readers of the gospel, not first in time, but placed first in our New Testament collection. For Matthew, unlike most of the other disciples who were working fishermen, could use a pen. And when he turned away for ever from his tax-gathering table, he carried his pen with him.

The last I must take space to mention as an unlikely man who received the respect of our Lord, was one of the two thieves along with whom He faced death. We know little of him and his colleague in crime, only that now they were both hanging, writhing in a hideous death. Dr Leslie Weatherhead contends that 'a thief can maintain *self-respect* while he evades the law. There is a certain tang in evading capture which ministers to a man's self-regard; but what self-respect can be left to a thief captured and crucified?' True – sadly true! But even at that late hour, Jesus had patient dealings with this outcast of humanity. Penitent, he is dealt with, listened to, and promised more than his most earnest request could have dreamed (Luke 23:39–43 A.V.). For there is no measuring the limits of gracious respect. This Jesus our Lord made plain – and it is worth reading through the gospels again, if only to add up instances. For if we are to be fully Christian today, you and I must know more than we often seem to do about this precious quality. Age has nothing to do with it – it reaches from life's beginning to life's end.

Respect is the right of the very youngest. George Macdonald was fond of saying: '*A parent must respect the spiritual person of his child*, for that, too, looks the Father in the face, and has an audience with Him, into which no earthly parent can enter even if he cared to desire it.'

At the far end of life, one needs the same measure of respect. Dr F. O. Bennet's widow lately gave me generous permission to quote from his little book, *The Tenth Home*. I like the passage concerning 'three elderly women, mesdames A., B. and C.', who in one small ward that had become available, occupied the three corner beds. (The letters stand for Atheist, Brethren and Catholic.)

By the infallible democratic method of a majority vote they could prove that each held erroneous views. But their spiritual fervour stopped short of this. They were good friends. Each regretted, but did not resent, that the others did not have the Truth. The only mobile one was Mrs A., the Atheist, and her speed was recorded not in miles per hour, but in hours per mile. Yet she would retrieve Mrs B.'s Bible from the floor, and Mrs C.'s rosary beads from behind the locker, and in each case put them on the table with a smile and just that deliberate delicacy of touch which is reverence itself. None of them was beyond voicing her opinion, or of administering an indirect rebuke of the others per medium of a conversation with a nurse, her voice raised sufficiently for the others to hear! Yet when one of the Brethren prayed at Mrs B.'s bed, or Mrs C. crossed herself in the presence of the priest, or Mrs A. wanted to know where Lot got his wife, the others kept silent. *It was the silence of respect.*

Jesus our Lord showed this precious quality in superlative degree – there is no record of His ever treating people as other than people. And this is the ongoing Christian challenge that faces you and me, today!

I BELIEVE . . . IN DAILY WORK

If you are ever in Sussex, as I have been several times, and you come to the church at the foot of Wolstonbury Hill, take time to look at the man with a spade there, and the man with a book, together bearing the words: 'Do it with thy might!' They represent work of a physical kind, and work of an intellectual kind. And there is no suggestion that one is more important than the other. The dictionary defines 'work' as 'an expenditure of energy, an application of effort to some purpose'. (Curiously, I had reached the day of my retirement before I looked it up. From my earliest youth, I had known well what 'work' was – and enjoyed it. Perhaps being born to grow up on a farm made it so.)

In these days of Women's Lib somebody is for ever telling a woman what she ought to be doing, when she is already doing what someone else told her she ought to be doing. It seems to me that we each do best the work of our own choosing, which we women claim possible these days: encouraging a seated toddler to accept one more mouthful of cereal; taking down dictation from a boss; making, or minding, a complicated piece of machinery; or giving service in nursing, chemistry, doctoring, law, social welfare, or in a dozen other modern contributions to life. It wasn't possible till relatively recent times – my mother enjoyed no such opportunity, not to mention her mother. At about that time, Charlotte Brontë was speaking up for many besides herself: 'I believe single women should have more to do – better chances of interesting and profitable occupation than they possess now. And when I speak thus, I have no impression that I displease God by my words; that I am either impious or impatient . . .' Bless her! Charlotte was tired of purposeless days, and the widespread custom of reviving fainting daughters with artificial expectation. The greater number of them, she knew, would never marry. 'Look at the numerous families of girls in this neighbourhood,' she wrote. 'The brothers of these girls are every one in business or in professions.'

The coming of World War I made a great difference – unhappily, it took a war to do it. Then G. K. Chesterton, with a chuckle, could write of young women, who for the first time knew themselves free of father's bounty, as they took office jobs, each declaring: 'I will not be dictated to' – *and forthwith became stenographers!*

During that same time, of course, man's work was changed, too, though less markedly. 'Once', as one keen observer, Percy Ainsworth, reminds us, 'the shepherd went to his flocks, the farmer to his field, the merchant to his merchandise. There are still flocks and fields and markets, but where are the leisure, grace and simplicity for him who has any share in the world's work? Men go out today to face a life shadowed by vast industrial, commercial and social problems. Life has grown complicated, involved, hard to understand, difficult to deal with . . . There is the danger that always lurks in things – a warped judgement, a confused reckoning, a narrowed outlook . . . The danger in the places where men toil is not that God is denied with a vociferous atheism; it is that He is ignored by an un-voiced indifference. *And thus the real battle of life is not the toil for bread. It is fought by all who would keep alive and fresh in their hearts the truth that man doth not live by bread alone.*'

Eyebrows were raised to hear an Archbishop of Canter-bury, Dr William Temple, say: 'It is a mistake to think that God is interested solely in religion.' He is interested in work; there is no forgetting our Lord's striking words: 'My Father worketh hitherto, and I work' (John 5 : 17 A.V.).

When God sent His Son to live the life of a man on earth, He made it possible for Him to work as a carpenter

at a bench in little Nazareth. His tools were simple enough
– I have spent time in that little town, watching a carpenter, and our Lord's tools would have been simpler still.
And in His day, He had to turn His hands to many a task
– from the cutting of the tree, to the fashioning and
finishing of ox-yokes, stools, chests, and children's toys.
When He put up the shutter for the last time Himself, and
another of the family took over, He went for the Baptism
of John. And there a voice from Heaven was heard, saying:
'This is My beloved Son, *in Whom I am well pleased.*'
'What had He done at that stage, to so please God?' one
asks. And the answer is, 'No preaching, teaching, or healing
– none of the special parts of what we call "His ministry".
He had done nothing but a decent piece of carpentry – His
work as a craftsman, a weekly worker.'

There is sincerity behind Charles Wesley's prayer:

> Son of the carpenter, receive
>   this humble work of mine;
> worth to my meanest labour give,
>   by joining it to Thine!

There are countless tasks today at which a woman, not to
speak of a man, in discipleship may serve. In a publication
called 'Careers: A Guide to the professions and occupations of educated women and girls' – taking five hundred
and fifty-odd pages – I found a list of present-day opportunities, a hundred and seventy four forms of work, in
alphabetical order, all the way from Accountancy to
Zoology. (And the first letter, 'A', would have surprised
Charlotte, a hundred years after her appeal. A woman
today might take up not only Accountancy but Advertis-
ing, Agriculture, Angora Rabbit Farming, Archaeology,
Architecture, Archive Work, Arts and Crafts, and Avi-
ation.) And I will not be surprised to find that list much
extended when I peruse the next edition. Listed in this

admirable Guide, from its first appearance (replacing the term 'governess', widely used in Charlotte's day and sometimes attended by a measure of humiliation) are extensions now of midwifery, general nursing and child care. Some of these women will do special work for the Church, as nuns, deaconesses or parish visitors. And much more is done voluntarily.

No woman today need feel apologetic about any work; and many are so highly qualified. A youth-leader, volunteer, or choirmaster, nevertheless, knows what the priest knows when he hangs up his surplice after Evensong, that there is no 'sacred' or 'secular' in God's service. And I'm always glad when divisions of this kind are fully recognized within the Church. I shall long remember some beautiful windows that make this plain, in the Parish Church of Hillsborough and Wadsley Bridge, in Yorkshire, showing men with their tools of the every-day – a farmer with his hayfork and a miner with his pick. (My only disappointment, and a very real one, lay in the fact that the stained-glass craftsman hadn't included a woman worker.) I am no feminist; but it was a right moment when I discovered the Lady Chapel in Liverpool's glorious new cathedral. Women alongside men and from every part of the social range were remembered there – down to Kitty Wilkinson, the washerwoman, who, inviting her neighbours to use her cottage washtub, helped to allay a dreaded cholera attack. Cleanliness she underlined as important to healthy family life; but many lacked the facilities. In time, Kitty managed to persuade the authorities to establish in Liverpool the first public baths and wash-houses in any English city. I was gratified to see, there in stained glass, this 'saint of the soap-suds', this humble worker for God (I copied her epitaph: *Indefatigable and self-sacrificing'* I could wish that many other types of women's work might be as generously recognized.)

It is wonderful to have work of one's own choosing to

offer to God, to offer to the world. Much goes bypassed, even that offered through the Church.

There are, nevertheless, some types of work that from the first have been unacceptable. Then, one might *not* serve as a gladiator, if he were Christian; nor as an incense-maker for heathen sacrifices; nor in any work as a servant – man or woman – that demeaned in any way one's fellows. And the same ought surely to be as true today. No young person ought to be encouraged to work in a brewery, a brothel, or in the drug-scene, amongst other undertakings.

Dr Rupert Davies, noted modern scholar, elaborates very tellingly the words of Jesus: 'My Father worketh hitherto, and I work.' 'God's creating work is still going on. Every baby born, every new invention, every idea that comes to life in someone's mind, every healthy development in the structure of human society, every poem or play or picture that catches something new about the meaning of life, every sculpture or building whose shape reveals or realizes another human possibility, is the work of the creative Spirit of God . . . God's work within the human person-ality, and in human relations, also continues. Every life redirected into useful channels, every conquest of a temptation or a demoralizing habit, every success in becoming a real, authentic person, no longer subject to the dominance of fashion, or prejudice, or someone else's possessive personality, every advance in personal relation-ships, is an example of this.'

It is one of the richest of human blessings to have work that is fulfilling – that one can show to God, and to one's fellows, as real service, that brings its own challenge, and uses one's own particular gifts and graces. An old-time prayer still rings true, and I find it often on my lips:

O Lord, renew my spirit that my work may not be a burden, but a delight.

AMEN

When the sky is momentarily overcast – by sickness, worry, death – there is nothing like memory. But one needs to know how to handle it. This secret made the Psalmist so level-headed, so level-hearted. Raising his voice in his dark moment, he was able to say: '*This* is my infirmity, but I will remember the years of the right hand of the most High' (Psalm 77:10 A.V.).

Any one of us who remembers only when a member of the family fell and broke a leg; or the year an investment failed; or one's favourite fruit tree was hopelessly blighted, is mis-using memory, he is only using it half-way. John Angell James took time every Saturday of his life to read aloud to his family the one hundred-and-third Psalm. Then his wife died. Suddenly, the sky was overcast and dark for the whole family. Father John hesitated for a moment, but only for a moment, for he already understood something of the dual ministry of memory. 'Notwithstanding what has happened,' he summoned courage to say, 'I see no reason for departing from our custom of reading: "Bless the Lord, O my soul, and *forget not all His benefits!*" '

From the beginning, God desired us men and women not only to remember the bitter experiences, but the good, rich, gracious ones as well. This is something that, one by one, we have to build up through all the years. And sometimes our memories are of very ordinary things. One made this little prayer:

> Thank God for trees,
> bird, blossom, breeze;
> And thank Him most for all of these –
> fun, frolic, cheers,

joy, laughter, tears –
And memory that
both sees and hears!

(Anon.)

I have a dear friend who has spells of wakefulness at night.
'And what do you do?' I asked her, 'take pills?' 'No,' she
answered me, 'I tell myself my body is getting rest anyway,
when I'm not thrashing about beneath the bed-clothes.
Sometimes, before I begin to lie still, I get up and make
myself a cup of tea, and get a biscuit, living alone as I do.
Then I lie quietly, and remember things – and I like to do
that. I learned a lot of things by heart, when I was young
– poems, and stories, and psalms, and passages of Scripture.
It's a pity that children are not encouraged to learn things
by heart these days. They're wonderful for when one can't
sleep.' I agree, though I'm not a wakeful person. And there
are other times when memory exerts a unique ministry,
too. I once spent many weeks in bed with a badly scalded
leg. When everybody was busy, I had time alone; but I
already had a memory well-stored with things I'd found
in books. I once lived alone, and worked on a church job
in a part of the country that had just suffered a devastating
bushfire, and all the tall trees stood black, stark skeletons.
Then I needed memories of green spring and summer
growth. I was once forced to spend much of two years on
my back with a grievous heart-condition – and I needed
memory then. I once spent days engaged in prison visitation, and in social work in the dullest back streets of a
great city during an economic depression – and I needed
memory then. It is one good thing to go forward and forget
– *but it's an even richer thing, at times, to go back, and
remember.*

I can't remember now when first I picked up some words
spoken by the great Dean Inge, or where; but I've never
forgotten them. Said he: *'There is so much that we have*

no right to forget!' There is! It was my lot to be born and grow up in a beautiful pastoral countryside. The hills and trees, and changing seasons there, remain with me still — something rich of God's giving! And now, when I chance to be wakeful, or have a solitary train journey or night flight, that might otherwise be dreary, I have the ministry of memory. I once carried a haversack around England, and slept nightly in Youth Hostel beds for a shilling each night. I once flew over a Swiss mountain in a thunder-storm, and that thunder-storm is not yet finished with for me. I once climbed into a bell-tower with a company of village bell-ringers — and those bells still ring for me. I can remember — whatever the weather, and wherever I am in this round world — the clear sky over the tall spire of Salisbury Cathedral, the tallest in England. In the dullest spot, I can see the ancient ongoing thread of the Pilgrims' Way that I tramped, down through the countryside into Canterbury town. I can see fellow trampers setting forth into the hills with heavy haversacks and bright faces; and King's College Chapel is always a reality; and I go over the big cities, that villages and beautiful bridges have brought me to. Dean Inge was right — he knew the secret of the Psalmist: 'There is so much that we have no right to forget!' Gracious old houses in the Black Forest; little children standing in a lamp-lit circle outside a door, sing-ing carols; gently ascending stone steps beyond the Chapter House of Wells Cathedral, hollowed through the centuries by countless feet.

And at the deepest level of all, of course, memory ministers to me. Paul might have passed on many impor-tant pieces of advice to young Timothy, setting out. It was plain to both of them, even at that point, that Timothy's ministry was to be adventurous and hazardous, too. What Paul said, as translated in our Moffatt version of the New Testament, couldn't have been a better word, by any reckoning. His words were simply: *'Never forget* Jesu

Christ risen from the dead!' (2 Timothy 2:8).

Some time ago, in a great celebration out of doors, I was called to speak a final word to a company in Queensland. It was the centenary of the Methodist Church in that immense State. I had previously spent weeks travelling over it, speaking in halls and churches; but this was different – in its magnificent way, the climax of all our gatherings. Six thousand of us poured out in procession to a little green spot where, a hundred years earlier, one young man, the Reverend William Moore, and his young wife had stood, pioneers of their church. Courage might have failed many, but it did not fail them. And now it was our turn – and what could I say in so short a time, that we might not fail in this age? Argument was useless, and there was no time for discussion. What I settled on, in what on reflection, I believe, was an inspired moment, was Paul's words to young Timothy, counting on the marvellous 'ministry of memory'. There were but two of us chosen as speakers, one man, and me, at a clear, resonant microphone under a sunny blue sky. For weeks we had been recounting the early days. Now, the vast company of which we were part was hushed – and the closing words they heard from my lips were those ageless words: '*Never forget* Jesus Christ risen from the dead!'

On that green spot, as in our church and private faith, much hinged on the ministry of memory! On the Resurrection of Christ!

I BELIEVE . . . IN WONDER

It can start from anywhere, from the smallest thing on to the largest. I found it first rising within me, as a small child, when I came across a four-leaf clover, a skip-and-a-jump along the little path from our home in Clover Road. Since growing up I've always believed in fostering this spirit of wonder in a child's heart, and seeking out ways to do it. For these are crowded days for most of us – we open our eyes to know ourselves surrounded by mechanical contrivances. We get up to wash in a basin with water flowing freely from a tap, far removed from a running stream; we eat food cooked on a gas or electric stove, that has little or nothing to do with the magic of fire and wood; we rush off to whatever will fill our day, along a bitumized path, or to a bus, tram or train, that we come to take for granted; we spend a lot of our day where the air is stirred by an electric fan, and lighting is caught in a little bulb. And our leisure is likely to be crowded with as many things: wireless sets, talk-back programmes, TV heroes and anti-heroes. When we get out of doors, it is mostly to join in games organized for us – not at all the same as lying beside a stream with its gurgling music in our ears, or in a field among the clover.

I was fortunate enough to hear one day the Irish author-artist-naturalist, Robert Gibbings – a great man in a great world – retell some of his experiences recorded in *Lovely is the Lee*. He had made a leisurely trip down the Lee, observing the sweet, natural things as he went. At one stopping place a letter reached him from Patrick Flannery of Ballinrobe. They had never met; but Patrick offered his boat on Lough Mask. 'So a few weeks later,' said Gibbings, joyfully, 'I stepped out at Ballinrobe, and he was there to meet me; warm and gentle, a man who, during a long life, *had never lost an opportunity to wonder.*' I like that.

> Lord, let me keep the glow of Wonder –
> At the starry host's unhurrying wheel,
> The drum-tapped tidings told by thunder,
> And the sea-bowl's moonlight of molten steel.
>
> (Anon.)

Knowledge, some say, drives out wonder from the world. But no, it is not so! Knowledge and wonder go hand in hand – and worship joins them. It is right that we should pray as some of us do, that by the inspiration of the Loving Spirit we may direct the thoughts of our children through curiosity to Wonder, through fairies to angels, through the imagination and delights of playtime, to the worship and joy of the Eternal!

One of my greatest grown-up experiences was standing on the rim of the Grand Canyon: two hundred and seven miles long, and more than a mile deep. But it was, I discovered, an experience of wonder that broke through statistics altogether – as all wonder does! From where I stood, silently gazing down, the mighty Colorado River could be seen winding its way like a tiny thread, around it the most dramatic natural sculpture in Creation, and constantly changing in mood. Early in the morning the Canyon appeared gentle, mist-shrouded, mysterious, developing soon into pinks and mauves, purples and deep blues. Later in the day it moved towards a rich honey-colour, then on to a cinnabar-red, with gold at sundown, the whole then soon seeming aflame! 'To really know the Canyon,' Francois Leydet – who knew it as well as anyone – had said, 'a man would need to have more than one life-time at his disposal.' In parts, the Creator's sculpturing-agents – river, sun, wind and rain – in all their moods, had cut away great walls. Where the Colorado wound its way sandy margins appeared, with tiny flowers growing, and small unhampered living creatures making their homes. There also was a tribe of Indians eking out its modest life-style. Every inch and aspect of the Grand Canyon was 'the stuff of Wonder'!

Few of us have a sufficiently big idea of God the Creator – but the Grand Canyon did much for me, widening and deepening my wonder. Said Isaiah, long ago: 'Have you not known? Have you not heard? The Lord is the everlasting God, the Creator of the ends of the earth. He does not faint or grow weary, his understanding is unsearchable!' (Isaiah 40:28 R.S.V.). Or if you are readier to lend an ear to one of our own time, then Professor Albert Einstein has this to say: 'The most beautiful, the most profound emotion we can experience, is the sensation of the mystical. It is the power of all true Science. He to whom this emotion is a stranger, *who can no longer wonder*, and stand rapt in awe, is as good as dead . . . This knowledge, this feeling is *at the centre of all true religiousness!*'

Wonder and Worship are kin. I might never again go back to the Grand Canyon, but I am for ever now a different person because once I stood there. Said J. B Priestley, coming, as I did, from our modern outside world 'My walk lasted hardly any ordinary time at all, yet it is almost like a remembered little life . . . As that great dome of rock brightened to gold and then slowly faded to bronze was stone and then fire and then stone again, some old hunger of the spirit was fed at last. *I felt wonder* . . . I had seen His handiwork, and I rejoiced!'

I felt exactly the same, and snatched at the words of the Psalmist, further back than Priestley's, to put it into speech 'Whatsoever the Lord pleased, that did he in heaven, and in earth, and in the seas, *and all deep places!*' (Psalm 135:6 A.V.). I had never looked into a deeper place of God', making than the Canyon – or into any one *so wonder-ful*'

And all life through it is not essential that the remarkable should serve my spirit – many common things that meet me in life are, I find, truly wonder-ful:

> When I reach old age, let me recall
> the green delights and pains of childhood —
> small leaf patterns dancing on a wall,
> wasp- and bee-stings never understood,
> and spring chestnut's sweet candelabra.
>
> Let the gold ambitious cock still crow,
> and laggard senses be roused at dawn —
> with all that Time has helped me to know
> in the crowded years since I was born,
> to share the height and depth of living.
>
> The Eternal salient in Time
> makes such things meaningful evermore —
> God's richest gifts amidst prose and rhyme,
> opening at last Death's hingéd door
> to a quality of Life unguessed!
>
> (R.F.S.)

Wonder we need, in this world! And Worship we need!
The architect of Truro Cathedral found words for his task,
words that I can never forget, when he said: 'My business is to think what will bring people soonest to their
knees.' That is, surely, as much the business of the builder
of the most modest church or chapel on earth — and the
leader of the most ordinary service of worship knows a like
call. One can worship, of course, in a barn — I have done
it; but it is easier to do so in a building beautifully
designed to be conducive to worship. Yet the building is
not all — there are some people who will saunter into the
greatest cathedral or church, saunter through, and saunter
out. To them it means nothing that God has done wonders
with human hearts there through the ages, spelling out, in
terms that humble men and women can understand, the

thought of His Majesty, the miracle of His love! It is a great loss, in any age, when we develop a sense of self-sufficiency, and fail to make a space for worship in our busy lives. Some remember young Eric Loveday, beloved Vicar of St Martin-in-the-Fields, London, saying as much in simple earnest words: 'When you abandon prayer and public worship, when you let your children do what they like on Sundays and teach them only science in the week, the only freedom you are seeking for yourselves and them is the freedom to sit down and be frightened of the world. *There is no substitute for the worship of God, conscious and spontaneous. None at all.* Clergymen', he was moved to add, 'do not tell people to come to church to stop them enjoying the world, but because they are obviously not enjoying the world as they were meant to. If all the arguments that you could worship God in the country, in music, in the laboratory, had been sound, we should have a happy people around us. We have done those things increasingly for years; and grown more terrified. If we had the courage, humility and energy to drop the Sunday paper, and spend ten minutes with the Bible, and Psalm 134, we should begin something towards supplying your greatest need and mine, the reality of God's world, the reality of His love for you, the secret which is open to anyone to discover, the secret of real worthwhile living. "Wonder, love, and praise!" the hymn calls it. And the means to it are here for us, in learning how to pray, to lean upon God: being one of a company of people worshipping Him and trying to work out His will in life.'

Adoration, penitence, thanksgiving, petition, dedication, all have a place in that experience. No one, like Jesus, ever understood what God was like, and what He most desired of man – and he went regularly to Worship. 'He came to Nazareth, where he had been brought up: and, *as his custom was*, he went into the synagogue on the sabbath day' (Luke 4:16 A.V.).

But worship, of course, is much more than routine. It is exposing one's whole self to reality. Pliny the Younger, whose dates are as early as AD 61–113, wrote officially, as Governor of Bithynia, to ask Emperor Trajan what he had to do with the Christians, people who were known to worship. He tells of their worship: 'As their custom was, they assembled on a fixed day before daybreak, shared a hymn to Christ as to a god, and together took an oath (*sacramentum*) . . . and these things done, strengthened in fellowship, dispersed to their ordinary concerns.'

The wonder is that to this very day worship continues – if as a mere duty to God – missing much that it might hold as the highest, most rewarding experience to us earth dwellers!

I BELIEVE . . . IN A LIGHT HELD HIGH

From the greatest experiences life offers, I have, of course, to come down to the commonplace. Though there is wonder of a kind in that, too, for Christianity is meant to be lived close to life. I have been in and out of many homes, and learned much there. I think of my visit to Chelmorton. Not only is it one of Derbyshire's highest villages, it is also one of the highest in all England. The elements have their way there, surrounding the homes with mists, or covering them at other times with snow. But it is the human element that makes Chelmorton memorable for me. One can think one's thoughts there among them — there is quietness enough for that.

I was guest in the home of John Morten, whose great-great-grandmother held a lantern for John Wesley when he came, at risk of life and limb, across the dark stretches of lonely country to preach in the village. Old 'Shop Grannie' kept a little shop there, and a room in her humble home was long used for preaching.

It is a proud family boast, for what old 'Shop Grannie' did for John Wesley, Wesley did in a more meaningful sense for many a one in a dark place: held high the lantern of God's Truth to make clear the way. And this is the privilege of us all, as Christians — whether parsons like John Wesley or priests, ministers, nuns, deaconesses, or also those who live in any kind of place where others live and struggle — including shop-keepers. It was so from the start. Early records mention fullers, slaves, parents, merchants — each laying hold of the opportunity to hold the light high. For this, they fully understood, was what Christ their Lord meant them to do. Did He not say: 'I am the

Light of the world'? – and as clearly go on to say: 'You are the light of the world . . . *let your light so shine!*' (John 8:12 and Matthew 5:14–16 A.V.).

Anyone who, like old 'Shop Grannie', has ever borne a light through the dark, knows that it does not do away with the darkness – *but it shows a way through it.* And that is something that I have to bear in mind, as I bear the lamp of God's light in Christ forward into any dark place. And there are many such parts of our world today, in personal and in public affairs. Here and there, often without warning, comes an accident, a cry of bewilderment, a grave illness, a tangled business relationship, an experience of intense loneliness, or a dark family relationship made up of subtle behaviour – and it is hard to find a clear, safe way ahead. It is at that moment when Christ's words come ringing clear: '*Let your light shine . . . and not to your own praise, but to the Glory of God, your Father!*' For it is God Who makes this possible, and supplies any light that is to be had in any dark circumstance; human effort, human wisdom is not enough. It is then that we need what He makes available in Christ – mediated through human friends, teachers, neighbours, 'lights' He has set near to our lives here and now.

Often the bearer of the Light is a humble person, with no more pretences than 'Shop Grannie' – a practical soul, bent on aiding God's purpose, in a place that she knows, and as she sees it. One of my favourite books in my growing up was a novel by Bess Streeter Aldrich, with its striking title – more and more striking, as I think of it – *A Lantern in Her Hand.* I read it then, once at least, every year; and it still has a place on my shelves, to read and to lend as I am able. It bears a verse by the poet Joyce Kilmer, who gave us that poem about God being the maker of a tree. The verse that Bess Streeter offers is every bit as close to life. It runs:

Because the road was steep and long,
   And through a dark and lonely land,
God set upon my lips a song,
   And put a lantern in my hand.

Any one of us who pretends to Christian discipleship can make that verse her own, his own, on the authority of our Lord's words: 'I am the Light of the World,' 'You are the light of the world . . . let your light so shine . . . to the glory of God your Father!' This in no sense is a contradiction, or a confusion, rather is it saying: the light is not your own creation; it is My gift, part of My very own nature. So it will prove sufficient. Hold it high, that others in a dark place may find their way home!

Another thing is that a light is not a rowdy, pretentious thing, *but a wordless witness*. So any one of us can bear the light entrusted to us. We may not be clever enough theologically to argue the things of God that have bearing on our journey through this world – but if they are real in our experience, through the mercy and love of Christ, we can witness to them by our faithful living. It might well be a silent affair, as silent as holding a lantern high, as old 'Shop Grannie' did, and in the realm of the spirit many of us have tried to do since. We are all capable of that much, in the life we live, in the place where we live, 'here and now'. It is a wonderful reality that to the glory of God it is so. We are each asked to accept the daily, nightly challenge. For nothing has ever happened to age it, excuse it, or spoil it: Christ's words still come to us, as excitingly beautifully as ever. And the experience of it is as vital: 'Let your light so shine!'

Dr H. H. Farmer reminds us, in *God and Man*, that our witness is as much as ever related to the time and circumstances in which we find ourselves. Says he: 'Being modern and speaking to modern minds, we must make a modern presentation of the Christian message. But we must be very alert to see that it is *the Christian message* we present, and that none of its distinctiveness is sacrificed to the desire to be "up to date".' Exactly! In the dark spot nothing takes the place of light – no clever psychological or philosophical jargon, no strange new Eastern notions. Christ alone is the Light of the World! Nobody else, in human experience here and now, has Himself claimed to be the Light of the World – or proved Himself to *be* that! This is the unique light that we carry, as Christians – not to our praise, but to the sole glory of God!

Each day dawns, each night comes – in human experience, as surely happens in the natural world about us, no one escapes – and to each comes the need of a light upheld. We are none of us sufficient in ourselves; nor is anyone else who shares this human experience with us. We all at some time come upon a dark patch, and need what Christ can make real to us, through the shining reality that He is in the life and spirit of someone else near enough to our lives to be effective. This can mean everything to one in the midst of a bewildering choice, a sense of estrangement, a frightening medical diagnosis, agitation about some coming obligation that seems too hard to face alone.

Christians who remain safely within the Church miss a great deal. For they are not called to be witnesses alone within the Church, not at all, but within the world. Said Christ to those who first knew themselves as His disciples: 'Ye shall be witnesses unto me both in Jerusalem [where they were], and in all Judaea [the next place out], and in Samaria [further out still], and unto the uttermost part of the earth [wherever there might be others living, and needing a Light upon the way]' (Acts 1:8 A.V.). As members of the Church, we are called to live outside the walls of the building we know, to carry a light to those outside, close at hand, and ever further away. The Rev. Arthur Whitham, one of the most beloved Methodist ministers and writers of our day, delighted to remind us that: 'Our religion begins as a domestic affair, and ends in a foreign policy; it first accepts a gift, and then proceeds to distribute it.' For nothing spreads like light from a lantern held high.

And the call is: *'Let your light shine'* – not somebody else's, but some light real to you, a gift from the great Light of the World to you, experienced and tested, and rejoiced in *by you*! Florence Allshorn liked to speak of an RAF pilot who said to a Christian with whom he came into contact: 'Don't try to help me or preach to me or tell me what I ought to think yet. Don't work for my salvation. *Show me yours!*' That's the simple secret, all anyone can do with a light: hold it high! It is one's witness that is unique, distinctive, unlike any other faith in this world – witness to Jesus Christ, above all, and to the glory of God! The very first Christians had no greater challenge, the greatest saints, the humblest sinners – it is still our privilege to do no more, no less, than keep our light high, and burning!

I BELIEVE . . . IN LIFE AFTER DEATH

Morning by morning the newspaper renews its face: its headlines and new items. We expect it – we live in a changeful world. But three columns are constant: Births, Deaths and Marriages.

We readers can do something about the first and third, but Death is outside our will to change. Between the first two, Birth and Death, an unexpected see-saw has occurred. In earlier days little or nothing was made of Birth in conversation, whilst Death was a centre of constant, often mournful speculation. Now, the order seems to be reversed. We speak and write much of Birth, especially underlining sex, and little or nothing of Death, as if it were less real. In the news columns it appears under its own name; but in that special three-fold heading, to which many readers turn first on opening the newspaper, an attempt is made to smudge over Death's reality. Notices speak of someone 'having lost a dear one', of the person named 'having passed on', or 'passed over'. Why is this, I find myself wondering? Is it because of a widespread sentimentality that provides – or is thought to provide – a screen of comfort at this time? Or is it a widespread fear of Death? 'I think it is the name that is so frightening,' said Lady Glenconner's child. 'I don't like to say it; it is so terrible, *Death*. I wish it wasn't called that! I don't think I should mind it so much if it were called *Hig*.'

But there is no dodging Death; this is not to be morbid, it's to be realistic. I was greatly taken by a recent Death notice in my newspaper – it was so natural. It was inserted by a Maori child, under the heading: 'Joseph, nana.' I read it thoughtfully, and cut it out. It read simply:

In loving memory of my darling Nana,
who left me on January 9.
Dear nana, how are you getting on. I miss you very much.
I hope you had a good Xmas. Sometimes
when I look at your photo it
makes me want to cry, but mummy
tells me you would not want me
to and some day I will meet you
again. Goodbye nana, I will never
forget you.
Love from your granddaughter
Te Aroha Perawiti. Te Kuiti.

I was struck by the child's acceptance of Death, and of awareness of Life after Death. I have no idea how old the little granddaughter was who submitted that notice to the newspaper, but it seems plain she believed that her beloved Nana still lives, and is capable of enjoying things like the keeping of Christmas. Theologically, I cannot in all honesty offer any proof that the festivals of the Church – Christmas, Easter, Whitsun, etc. – are celebrated in the Great Hereafter; that is just one of the many things we do not know. It must have sustained many in their thinking of Death to have no less a loved and trusted person than the great William Temple, Archbishop of Canterbury, shortly before his own early, lamented death, say: 'There is nothing in the world of which I feel so certain. I have no idea what it will be like, and I am glad that I have not, as I am sure it would be wrong. I do not want it for myself as mere continuance, but *I want it for my understanding of life.*'

It is easy, of course, to become facetious in the presence of this great mystery. Little Te Aroha avoids this altogether – life 'Here' and 'There' is all of a piece to her. The same natural acceptance is in the statement of the

Rev. Len Barnett, in a book for modern youth: 'I believe in Heaven. It makes sense of earth.' These are but two parts of God's gift to us, both of them indubitably linked. Among the facetious I recall a workman I chanced on with a pick, outside a damaged church in a side street in central London. As I stood a moment examining a curious example of the monumentalist's art, toppled amid chunks of stone, the workman's question met me: 'Lady, do you understand this?' 'Not altogether,' I had to reply, 'but my guide-book tells me it represents a certain artist's idea of Heaven. And as you can see, among these ascending bodies, there aren't any women – they are all men.' 'Well,' answered the interested workman, with a twinkle, 'I think he's got something there!' And so we parted.

Talk of golden crowns, the playing on harps, and of golden streets through Heaven, is little better, if these symbols (appearing in the Bible's last book, for a symbol-loving people) are taken literally. We know so little, but there is one thing we do know: in the Life Hereafter we shall be delivered from material conditions.

Some other answers to our questioning we can also be sure of: we shall be relieved of our physical pains, weari-nesses, and wants, that learned writers call 'the burden of the flesh'. We shall also be relieved of our present restric-tions, disappointments and faulty knowledge. We shall be done with the transient, and the partly-comprehended. And temptation – tied up with so much of our selfish longings, and our physical bodies – will also be at an end. Bodies, as we know them, can have no place in Heaven. The confusing terms in the Apostles' Creed, which asks each of us to affirm: 'I believe in the resurrection of *the body*', means in actuality: 'I believe in the resurrection of *the personality*' – not in my ten-stone-one of human bones, flesh, heart, blood, nerves. I wish the Creed said more exactly what it means. Dr William Barclay says that the word 'body' is retained as 'conserving the truth that salvation is the salvation of the total man, that personality survives, that after death we are neither obliterated nor absorbed into the Divine, but that we remain individual personalities'. All the lovely qualities of love, unselfishness, tolerance, sincerity, courage, joy, and the rest that make up a full personality, will at last be supreme. We cannot think of Heaven as a literal place, like Earth is a place, but rather as a state. This may be very close to meaningless for some of us, because we are so bound to things physical and material.

In Heaven, I believe we shall be free of the limitations of these bodies, young or old, well, fit, or disfigured, supported by calipers, or artificial hips, and fitted out with spectacles, hearing-aids, and other temporary but welcome helps of this modern age. Death for many, hindered by 'unwilling bodies', can only be a relief from what this world means for them, and for those who tend them; though we each cling to what we know, in the presence of the unknown, we are made that way. Julian Green, for all his modern experience, has said: 'I have always been awkward at putting flowers on graves, because I believe that those we once loved are now elsewhere!' Though flowers, I am bound to say, do help, in expressing the idea of life and beauty from apparent death, as when bulbs speak to us in spring; and flowers of any kind, at any time, soften the bareness and grimness of a crematorium or grave-side without some symbol of friendly, loving care. I would never want my tired-out body, or that of anyone dear to me, to be laid aside without flowers. For however strongly and deeply and happily one believes in 'Life after Death', as I do, there is still the natural shock of Death's presence to deal with, and the resultant change in the on-going life pattern of those left, as well as the loss of the everyday love of the departed one – all splendid things. And one would miss the response to one's call: 'Look at this!' And one would miss the wholesome refreshment of laughter

I tell myself, nevertheless, that I need not be embarrassed by tears, for all that I am not naturally a tearful person. A recent writer, in a medical journal that came my way, was at pains to point out that part of the reason why women live longer than men is that they know 'how to shed tears'. Tensions are dealt with that way.

In the experience of Death – one's own, or the reception of news of another's death – of course the central reality is *the message, and the Resurrection of our Lord Himself!* His words to each of His disciples were: 'Let not your heart be troubled: ye believe in God, believe also in Me' (John 14). But I need not quote in full that loved chapter – so many of our Bibles fall open naturally at that place. The Good News Bible translates His words: 'Do not be worried and upset. Believe in God and believe in Me. There are many rooms in my Father's house, and I go to prepare a place for you. I would not tell you this if it were not so. And after I go and prepare a place for you, I will come back and take you to myself, so that you will be where I am' (and later, as in verse 19) '*Because I live, ye also will live.*'

In *The Christian Replies* (Epworth Press), Dr Leslie Davidson, as editor, draws a thoughtful balance as an outcome of studious New Testament reading: 'For Christians the most impressive evidence is the teaching of Jesus. Jesus clearly believed and taught that good and bad alike survive Death, and that their destinies in the Life Beyond depend directly on the aims that they have pursued here. He warned His hearers of the gathering of the wheat into God's garner, and the rejection of the tares; told them of the separation of the sheep from the goats, and spoke of the blessedness of the faithful and the misery of the workers of iniquity. These', added Dr Davidson, 'are all symbols to convey the survival of essential personality. In the parable of the rich fool, and the story of Lazarus and the rich man, Jesus exposed the folly of living as though this life were all. The same kind of teaching is found in the writings of the Apostles. It is obvious that belief in a future life is absolutely bound up with the Christian religion.'

Jesus – in His teaching, and in His facing Death Himself – never once argued about Life after Death, He assumed it. Said He: 'If it were not so, I would have told you' (John 14:2 A.V.). 'Fear not them that kill the body', He said on another occasion, 'but are not able to kill the soul' (Matthew 10:28 A.V.).

And putting His unquestioned faith to the final test, as Death – in one of its cruellest manifestations – met Him on a Cross in a public place, His words as He died were: *'Father,' (He was Father, still) 'into Thy Hands I commit my spirit!'* (N.E.B.).

Jesus there, did not evade Death – He conquered it! After that, how should I fear to die? *'I believe . . . in Life after Death!'*

I BELIEVE . . . IN BEGINNINGS

Beginnings are so important, not only in words furnished – they go on all through life, walking, reading and so on. I heard Dr John Foster, Professor of Ecclesiastical History in the University of Glasgow, speak of this over the Scottish Home Service, very simply, very charmingly: 'If we can't look back and understand things in our own childhood,' said he, 'we get an occasional help to understanding from our children. I'll never forget one morning when a five-year-old bounced into my bed. He was at that stage, not uncommon among intelligent children, learning to read; his reading was limited to words of one syllable, and he was bored to death with the book – you know, "Fred has a cat in the van" – and ready to try anything.

'His hand reached out for the book on my bedside table. It was a New Testament, and it opened at the first chapter of St John's Gospel. He began: "In the beginning was the Word, and the Word was God . . . And the Word became flesh and dwelt among us." Verse after verse, he read, with only an occasional "What's that, Daddy?" He was reading the most sublime words, most of them only one syllable – nearly as easy as "Fred has a cat in the van". *But if that five-year-old lives to be a hundred, he won't have finished exploring those words and their meaning. The Christian religion is itself like that, and I have proved it so* – so easy that anybody can begin; but there is so much in it that you never get to the end.' (Though you finish a book like this present one, and many more.)

That's its glorious truth: it reaches the end of life here, on to Life in another world. John put it in good words: '*Now* are we sons of God, and it doth not yet appear what we shall be' (1 John 3:1 A.V.). A fascinating and stimulating thought!

Some beginnings, though not all, are easy. It's the going-on which 'yieldeth the true glory'. It may even be easy to read a profound passage from the Bible, as Dr Foster's five-year-old discovered; it may even be easy, in time, to respond to the appeal of the Supreme Lord and Master of Whom that wonderful passage speaks, to fall in love with Him, and become a Christian. It is even easy to mouth that lovely prayer, which many others, setting out, have used: 'Go before us, O Lord, in all our doings with Thy most gracious favour, and further us with Thy continual help, that in all our works, *begun, continued and ended in Thee, we may glorify Thy holy name, and finally, by Thy mercy, obtain Everlasting Life.*'

My best-loved poem on this beckoning prospect is by a fellow Christian, Percy Ainsworth. (It is longer than I usually like to quote, but I can't decide which verses to leave out, thereby leaving you wondering which ones I have omitted.) Of the Life Everlasting, he writes:

It will not meet us where the shadows fall
    Beside the sea that bounds the Evening Land;
It will not greet us with its first clear call
    When Death has borne us to the farther strand.

It is not something yet to be revealed –
    The everlasting life – 'tis here and now;
Passing unseen because our eyes are sealed
    With blindness for the pride upon my brow.

It calls us 'mid the traffic of the street,
    And calls in vain, because our ears are lent
To these poor babblements of praise that cheat
    The soul of heaven's truth, with earth's content.

It dwells not in innumerable years;
　　It is the breath of God in timeless things —
The strong, divine persistence that inheres
　　In love's red pulses and in faith's white wings.

It is the power whereby low lives aspire
　　Unto the doing of a selfless deed,
Unto the slaying of a soft desire,
　　In service of the high, unworldly creed.

It is the treasure that is ours to hold
　　Secure, while all things else are turned to dust;
That priceless and imperishable gold
　　Beyond the scathe of robber and of rust.

It is a clarion when the sun is high,
　　The touch of greatness in the toil for bread,
The nameless comfort of the Western sky,
　　The healing silence where we lay our dead.

And if we feel it not amid our strife,
　　In all our toiling and in all our pain —
This rhythmic pulsing of immortal life —
　　Then do we work and suffer here in vain.

Life, after our beginnings, is all of a piece, 'Here and There'. And much is like that in this life. It is not a matter of one beginning, neatly in place — we are always being confronted with new ones; life holds that kind of surprise all the way. This is how it comes to us from God, sometimes very simply. Paul found this true of his call to carry the Gospel to Europe. A man, it seemed to him, stood calling: 'Come over to Macedonia, and help us!' That was all, as simple as that! Paul had been held up by a recurring spell of ill health, a fever, some think, like malaria, since he travelled at times in unhealthy parts. But health was no excuse to Paul – one of the most exciting 'beginnings' of all his days awaited him in that situation.

Some think 'the man calling' may have been Dr Luke; certainly Paul was no longer alone – from this time on, we get the 'we' passages in the story. Some offer what they call 'proof' that Dr Luke was himself a Macedonian; others refer to this only as 'an attractive theory'. But there is no doubt whatsoever that it was pivotal in the spread of the Christian Good News: a 'beginning'.

Paul sailed from Troas to Philippi. But on arrival, he and his colleague must have thought their reception an anti-climax, to say the least; no great multitude awaited them, just a few women gathered for a meeting for prayer down by the riverside. A pretty slim beginning it looked for the evangelization of a continent! Yet, that day, for the first time ever, *the Gospel reached Europe!* Ever afterwards, world history was to be different – and yours and mine, 'Here and Now!'

This should be encouragement enough – Philippi hadn't so much as a synagogue to start with. Yet God's purpose was realized: a 'beginning' took root in the world of men! Most were ordinary enough – like ourselves, we rejoice to think; there weren't many brilliant minds like Paul's. And that, I believe, is still true of many of God's purposes. I find encouragement at this point, and know joy in ending this book that we have shared, rather surprisingly, with 'beginnings'. We have read much together – but all of life lies offering us adventure 'Here and Now!'

If God is not like Jesus Christ —
to many of us He is incredible.
If He is like Jesus Christ, He is
irresistible.

Dr W. R. Malby

ACKNOWLEDGMENTS

The author acknowledges her indebtedness for use of the following material:

Two extracts from the work of Dr James S. Stewart

The poem 'Silent at Joseph's side He stood' by Phyllis Hartnoll

An extract from Dr H. H. Farmer's *The World and God*, Nisbet & Co. Ltd

The poem 'There is a closeness in the Fellowship of Christian Folk' by Asa Johnson

Two extracts from the work of Percy Ainsworth, by kind permission of the Epworth Press

Also available in Fount Paperbacks

The Holy Spirit
BILLY GRAHAM

'This is far and away Graham's best book. It bears the stamp of someone who has seen everything, and then has worked painstakingly and carefully in making his own assessment . . . The Christian world will be reading it for many years to come.'

Richard Bewes,
Church of England Newspaper

To Live Again
CATHERINE MARSHALL

The moving story of one woman's heart-rending grief and of her long hard struggle to rediscovery of herself, of life, of hope.

A Man Called Peter
CATHERINE MARSHALL

The story of a brilliantly successful minister and of a dynamic personality. Told by his wife, it is also the story of their life together; a record of love and faith that has few equals in real life.

The Prayers of Peter Marshall
CATHERINE MARSHALL

'This is a truly wonderful book, for these prayers are a man speaking to God – and speaking in a way that involves listening for an answer.'

British Weekly

Fount Paperbacks

Fount is one of the leading paperback publishers of religious books and below are some of its recent titles.

- ☐ SQUARE WORDS IN A ROUND WORLD Eric Kemp 95p
- ☐ THE HOLY SPIRIT Billy Graham 95p
- ☐ REACHING OUT Henri Nouwen 95p
- ☐ DEATH & AFTER: WHAT WILL REALLY HAPPEN?
  H. J. Richards £1.25
- ☐ GO AN EXTRA MILE Michael Wood 95p
- ☐ HAPPY FAMILIES Anthony Bullen 95p
- ☐ THE NEW INQUISITION? SCHILLEBEECKX AND KÜNG
  Peter Hebblethwaite £1.25
- ☐ CHRISTIANITY AND OTHER RELIGIONS
  John Hick & Brian Hebblethwaite £1.50
- ☐ TOWARDS THE DAWN Clifford Hill £1.25
- ☐ THE POPE FROM POLAND John Whale £1.50
- ☐ THE FAITH OF AN ANGLICAN Gilbert Wilson £2.95
- ☐ PRAYER FOR PILGRIMS Sheila Cassidy £1.50

All Fount paperbacks are available at your bookshop or news-agent, or they can also be ordered by post from Fount Paperbacks, Cash Sales Department, G.P.O. Box 29, Douglas, Isle of Man, British Isles. Please send purchase price, plus 10p per book. Customers outside the U.K. send purchase price, plus 12p per book. Cheque, postal or money order. No currency.

NAME (Block letters) _____

ADDRESS _____

_____

_____